This is the second book in our Darwin Anniversary Book Cycle. To honor the 200th Anniversary of Darwin's birth in 2009, we are publishing six books to cover the startling new understanding of Darwin, his theory of evolution, and the all-too-often ignored or forgotten work of progressive scientists over a century that corroborate and expand this new understanding and its major implications for science and society. Titles are: *Bankrolling Evolution. Measuring Evolution. Darwin's Lost Theory. Darwin on Love. The Derailing of Evolution. Telling the New Story.*

See back pages of this book for further information about worldwide events during the Darwin Anniversary and brief descriptions and core book endorsements by leading scientists and educators.

Ben Franklin

Benfranklin@benjaminfranklinpress.com
www.benjaminfranklinpress.com

Measuring Evolution

By the author

The Healing of a Nation
The Leadership Passion
The Knowable Future
The Sphinx and the Rainbow
The Partnership Way (with Riane Eisler)
An Arrow Through Chaos
Darwin's Lost Theory of Love
The Story of a Family
The Evolutionary Outrider, Editor
The Great Adventure, Editor
Bankrolling Evolution

MEASURING EVOLUTION

A User's Guide to the Health and Wealth of Nations

DAVID LOYE

Benjamin Franklin Press
Darwin Anniversary Edition

Cover images: In the background, map of the famous voyage of Darwin's Beagle circling the earth for soundings of safe harbors for international trade. Inset image: the statue of Justice on top of Old Bailey in London—which differs from all other statues of justice in having no blindfold. Look closely and you will see that in our version she also holds a measuring stick rather than the traditional sword.

Published by
The Benjamin Franklin Press
A BFPress First Edition

1. Management science. 2. Politics. 3. Evolution. 4. Philanthropy

Cover by John Mason. Production: Cassandra Gallup-Bridge. Back cover photo: Don Eddy.

For more information about Benjamin Franklin Press books
www.benjaminfranklinpress.com
benfranklin@benjaminfranklinpress.com
The Benjamin Franklin Press, P.O. Box 222851, Carmel, CA 93923
Phone: 831-624-6037. Fax: 831-626-3734.

Copyright © 2007 David Loye
All rights reserved.
ISBN-13: 978-0-9789827-1-3
ISBN-10: 0-9789827-1-1

Dedicated to

Hazel Henderson and Alan Kay,
and to the memory of
Silvan Tomkins, Milton Rokeach,
Klaus Riegel, Mary Henley, Francis Gramlich,
Hadley Cantril, Ashley Montagu,
old friends at Educational Testing Service,
and the Golden Age of
Psychological Measurement

CONTENTS

One	The Social and Scientific Background to the Development of The Global Sounding	1
Two	A Full Spectrum, Action-Oriented Theory and Global Sounding Indicators	11
Three	Pilot Test of the Potential Global Effects of Regressive American Policies	18
Four	How to Use It *I*: The Global Sounding Measure with Basic Matrix and Blank Forms for Use by Decision-Makers in Business, Government, Politics, Science, Education, the Media, Nonprofit and Religious Organizations, and Philanthropists and Foundations	25
Five:	How to Use It *II*: Examples with Illustrative Forms for Use by Decision-Makers in	30
	Business	33
	Government	40
	Politics	48
	Science	56
	Education	65

	The Media	71
	Nonprofit Organizations	80
	Religious Organizations	87
	Philanthropists and Foundations	93
	Overview	99
Six:	Global Healing: The Challenge to Money, Science, Sense, and Sanity	101

End Documents 109

The Global Sounding Moral Code	111
The Code	115
Derivation of the Code	120
Bush Policy Violations of the Code	126
A Brief, Informal History of Measures of Global Well-Being	131
Social Science pioneers	132
Futurist movement	133
Evolutionary Systems Scientific movement	135
Human potentials movement	137
Quality of Life Indicators and Measures of Global Well-Being	139
The Women's movement	144
Psychiatric measures	146
Moral measures	148
Spiritual measures	150
Action context	153

The Scientific and Political Grounding for the Sounding	155
Further Developmental Considerations	165
The Problem of a Single Indicator for Cultural Evolution	169
A Brief History of the General Evolution Research Group	173
The Toronto Manifesto	191
The Darwin Project	194
The Lovelock Statement of Global Urgency	205
Notes and References	211
The Darwin Anniversary	215
The Darwin Anniversary Book Cycle	224
Pre-Publication Reviews	226
About the Author	234

ONE   THE SOCIAL AND SCIENTIFIC BACKGROUND TO DEVELOPMENT OF THE GLOBAL SOUNDING

Thousands of nuclear missiles—any one of which can within minutes obliterate 10 million of us. The vast ice masses at the North and South poles melting through global warming. The consequent rising of the seas threatening to destroy our earth's great coastal cities and entire islands. The widening gap between rich and poor, the proliferation of war, terrorism, famine, genocide.

All this and much more has made it evident to the buyers, readers, and users of this little handbook—that is, those of us lucky enough to be reasonably well informed, who care for human evolution and the well-being of life on this planet—that we face a life or death situation for all we value.

We confront what has become obvious to rapidly increasing numbers of us—that worldwide we face increasingly urgent questions about the present policies of governments, political parties, corporations, banks and other financial institutions, as well as science, education, religions, foundations and other non-profit organizations.

The basic question is to what extent do their present policies and actions drive us toward the "health and wealth of nations"?

Or—and generally this is without malice or any intention to do so, simply by the nature of being caught in the paradigms of earlier stages of evolution—do they further drive us toward destruction?

In other words, do they drive our species forward, hold us in check, or drive us backward in human evolution?

In the case of all that threatens our health and wealth as individuals, medical science has developed such useful tools as the thermometer for reading temperature, the sphygmomanometer for reading blood pressure, or the Snellen or other eye charts for reading the degree to which we can see with accuracy rather than distortion. This makes it possible for doctors to diagnose what ails us and do something about it.

The question that led to the development of the Global Sounding is whether equivalent tools can be invented to deal with what has become a life-threatening illness for our species.

That is, as with use of the thermometer with individuals, can something comparable be developed to initiate, guide, and monitor the healing of groups, communities, regions, and nations?

Darwin and the Development of the Global Sounding

The name Global Sounding comes from Darwin's famous voyage of the Beagle. Originally, this ship was commissioned by the British navy to circle the world to obtain *soundings* indicating peaceful harbors and safe channels for navigation through the hidden rocks and reefs.

As is well known, this became the ship and the voyage that opened Darwin's eyes to the vision that became, in *Origin of Species,* the biological foundation and first half for his theory of evolution. But we can see now how uncannily the mission of the Beagle also foreshadowed the vision in *The Descent of Man* and his early notebooks of the social

MEASURING EVOLUTION

and systems scientific—and, above all, morally-oriented and action-oriented—second and completing half for his theory.

It is this full and completed theory, integrating both halves, upon which the development of the Global Sounding is based.[1]

In the form of surveys, reports, and measures many attempts have been made by psychologists, sociologists, and other social scientists to develop measures for what either benefits or ails us socially and globally. To provide the background for optimal understanding and use of our new measure, in our End Documents you will find a brief history of these fascinating ventures. Because of the exciting surge of hope they raise out of what otherwise so often seems a hopeless time, I urge you to read this End Document (page 131) story of the worldwide development of measures of, in effect, the "rocks and shoals" of global sickness and the "safe harbors" of global health, or of global well-being.

Some of these measures are already widely in use, excellent in accomplishing what they've been designed to do, doing good in the world. But by and large either their complexity or isolation to one speciality or another leaves the need open for our new kind of measure.

In other words, there's a need for a new kind of relatively simple instrument for multi-level universal use by the so-called layman and laywoman as well as the experts. We need a measure, above all, based on an updated and expanded "full spectrum," moral-oriented and action-oriented theory of evolution.

We need this to provide us with a reasonably well-grounded scientific guide past the "rocks and shoals" threatening to swamp the human venture to the much better future we need for long term planetary viability and species survival.

Prior to recent decades, the task of constructing the kind of measure that is needed would almost certainly have been impossible. But the rise of the new field of evolutionary systems science—in which the General Evolution Research Group described in our End Documents was one of many pioneers—has long pointed toward the eventual development of the Global Sounding as, in effect, a global "thermometer" for monitoring the health and welfare of our species.

Such an invention is now within the capability of science for four reasons that, while technical, are vital for us to understand at this critical juncture in the evolution of our species as well as all other life on this planet.

The New Advantages of Evolutionary Systems Science

A first advantage of the new field of evolutionary systems science is that it both emerges from and embraces the late 20th century thrust of chaos, complexity, and earlier cybernetic theory.

This powerful advance for our understanding of our world first emerged out of an exploration of the subterranean dynamics of chemistry,[2] the physics and mathematics of weather prediction,[3] and, earlier, the mathematical roots for computer science.[4] But then in a move—in which I am admittedly proud to claim a very small part[5]—it expanded out of natural science into the vast territory that opens up with the shift to social science, the humanities, and theology at the vastly expanded level for our species.

A second advantage for evolutionary systems science is that its approach, or core methodology, forces one to learn the languages (e.g., the math as well as the so-called jargon) that today separate both natural and social science into often combative feudal territories of rigidly-bounded and fiercely-guarded separate scientific baronies.

Thus, this new holistic science, as in a sense both insider and outsider to whatever the problem is at hand, puts one in a better position to independently assess what ails us.

It also allows one to scientifically legitimize a hitherto seemingly impossible but vital need for science. By providing a way to perceive logical points of consensus underlying all the arguments—and to thus transcend the controversy that dogs all fields—it provides a way to anticipate the agreements that after much wrangling the separate baronies of science as a whole will most likely arrive at over possibly many decades.

This, as we'll see, is crucial in settling the critical matter of viable indicators of evolutionary progression versus regression.

A third advantage of the new field is that, in freeing itself to step aside from or rise above the academic battles and customary wrangling of the experts, it allows one to draw upon the unclouded power of *direct perception*. All too often foolishly devalued by academics, this, I'm delighted to note, is what is commonly referred to as common sense.

The fourth advantage—obviously vital now as the threat to planetary sustainability increases—is the *action tradition* for evolutionary systems science. From the pioneering of founders of the field, such as Kurt Lewin in psychology, Kenneth Boulding in economics, Harold Lasswell in political science, and Erich Fromm in social psychiatry, this is the conviction that, on gaining new knowledge that can improve our human situation, *one has the responsibility to act*—rather than sit by and wait for approval or for others to act.

That is, rather than being only the supposedly pure, objective, and value-free observer and reporter of what is happening to our species, a greater responsibility takes over.

Forging the link between progressive science and progressive social, economic, political, educational, and religious policy becomes the highest rather than the lowest of priorities for democracy and all other progressive goals for evolution.

The Imperative of Imperatives: Moral Advancement

The fifth and greatest advantage of this new field of science and its potential for the construction of a global "thermometer," however, is the new power it offers for shoring up what continues to be—even after the thousands of years we've been given to improve our situation—the pivotal weakness for our species on this planet.

Evolutionary systems science offers us new hope for a way to strengthen the presently weak and often entirely missing *moral* perspective in science and society.

It further offers a new way to put the wasteful and senseless old conflict between religion and science behind us. It gives us a way to raise up and untangle what has so often been woefully degraded and mangled by the regressives and the status quo-ites for both parties.

This was the perspective for the founders of social and systems science, such as Immanuel Kant in cognitive science, John Stuart Mill in economics, Sigmund Freud in psychology, Emile Durkheim in sociology, Jean Piaget in child psychology and education, and most striking in the case of his long ignored early and late work, of Charles Darwin—but unfortunately it has been of little or only token or peripheral concern to most of their successors.[6]

MEASURING EVOLUTION

As Darwin wrote over 100 years ago in *The Descent of Man*, "The moral faculties are generally and justly esteemed as of higher value than the intellectual powers."

In other words, in tune with the founders, a basic requirement for the scientific development of a "thermometer" to advance global healing is to encourage science—as well as religion—to become *vastly more effective morally sensitive advocates for humanity.*

This is why I feel that just as important as identifying the basic indicators for evolutionary advance and basic indicators for evolutionary regression is the translation in the End Documents for this book of the Global Sounding into its companion Global Sounding Moral Code.

The Scientific Sine Qua Non for Global Healing: A Full Spectrum, Action-Oriented Theory of Evolution

Out of the research, writings, and discussions of evolutionary systems scientists over the past thirty years or so, two books co-authored first by a dozen of us and then by another dozen of us—*The Great Adventure: Toward a Fully Human Theory of Evolution* (SUNY Press, 2004) and its predecessor *The Evolutionary Outrider: The Impact of the Human Agent on Evolution* (Praeger, 1998)—took two particularly useful steps in this direction.[7]

In line with the reconstruction for Darwin's long ignored vision for the completion of his theory of evolution, *The Evolutionary Outrider* probes the evolutionary activist perspective necessary for understanding the scientific basis for global healing. *The Great Adventure* then develops the case for going beyond the overwhelming 20th century fixation on the physics, chemistry, and biology of evolution to develop a "full spectrum," action-oriented theory of evolution.

To indicate the scope and quality of work behind these two books—which contain over 600 references, in turn providing both the launch point and a scientific legitimization for construction of the Global Sounding—it is important to know these books grew out of the perspective and works of the unusual multinational and multidisciplinary constituency of two groups of scientists and educators concerned with the task of updating and advancing evolution theory.

Back in the Cold War days, when the world faced the hair trigger possibility of all-out nuclear war between the U.S. and the Western Bloc and the Soviet Union and the Eastern Bloc, a small group of scientists from both sides secretly met behind the Iron Curtain in Budapest to see if they could form a joint project to head off the threatened nuclear showdown. Fired up by the excitement of the early development of chaos theory, the goal was to accelerate the development of a theory of evolution that might be used to guide humanity out of the social chaos of our time, past the nuclear threat, to a peaceful and better future.

Following this meeting, two years later in 1986 we met again to form the General Evolution Research Group to actively pursue the original goal. In symposia chiefly throughout Europe, as our membership expanded to include scientists from other disciplines and nations, we presented and published hundreds of papers and staffed and maintained a quarterly journal. For over a decade we even managed to publish a regular book series providing a forum for thousands of more studies from scientists throughout the world bearing on the development of this new perspective on evolution.

The story is told in more detail and at greater length in our End Document A Brief History of the General Evolution Research

MEASURING EVOLUTION

Group—or GERG, as it became known.

Out of this effort, in 2004 members of GERG and other concerned scientists and educators formed The Darwin Project (www.thedarwinproject.com). As again detailed in our End Documents, the purpose of this venture was and is to expand the teaching of evolution at all levels of education beyond the present narrow focus on the physics and biology of evolution to include the woefully neglected social and systems scientific, or "superstructural" cultural levels of evolution, which now shape the destiny and fate of our species and this planet.

An important summation and turning point for GERG came at the turn of the year into the 21st century. In 2000, members of GERG and the International Society for Systems Science (ISSS) met during the World Congress of the Systems Sciences in Toronto to take stock of where matters stood for "action science" and the comparatively new field of evolutionary systems science. The end result of two forums and a general discussion—highly critical of the failure of science to move with the needed speed in both directions—was the Toronto Manifesto (see End Documents) and publication of our papers first in a special issue of the GERG Journal *World Futures: The Journal of General Evolution*, and then publication by the State University of New York (SUNY Press) in *The Great Adventure: Toward a Fully Human Theory of Evolution*.

In keeping with the emphasis for the Toronto World Congress, *The Great Adventure* focuses on what a "full spectrum," action-oriented theory of evolution should look like. Then, most critically, it explores how we may transcend the contentious divisions and lag within all fields of science, and globally get together and *actively build the full spectrum, action-oriented theory.*

Specifically, the book shows how, with only a tiny investment in comparison to the billions now spent on armaments and wars, this can actually be done—and still in time to stave off global disaster. With an outline of curricula for doing this, the book shows how internet distance learning can be used to bring together a new worldwide involvement of students with teachers and action-oriented scientific mentors, to build the kind of action-oriented guide we urgently need for expediting the advance of human evolution.

Given this background and prelude to the development of the Global Sounding, we'll next take a look at specifically what a "full spectrum," action-oriented theory of evolution would look like, and how this new perspective has been used to develop the Global Sounding.

TWO A FULL SPECTRUM, ACTION-ORIENTED THEORY AND GLOBAL SOUNDING INDICATORS

Sometimes it seems that much of the money and energy going into science is spent on keeping it bottled up in a scientific monastery. The sacred goal for this monastery, it appears, is to avoid the difficulties of having to deal with the raw needs and painful realities of the world beyond the monastery walls for as long as possible.

This, however, seems to be largely a function of whether what the outside world wants from the monastery is the science for maintaining things as they are—which is eagerly encouraged and heavily rewarded; or the science for changing things as they are, which on emergence so often faces being ignored—or clubbed and shot down.

A core perspective for our book *The Great Adventure: Toward a Fully Human Theory of Evolution* (SUNY Press, 2004) is shown by the following sketch of the roots, trunk, and branches for a "tree of evolution"—which seems to take the form of a traditional "Christmas tree," with the bright angel of ACTION at the top.

In other words, this is a sketch of the relatively simple view of life on this earth that seems to underlie the confusion and controversy of what is, and what we should be doing about, evolution.

DAVID LOYE

Action
Consciousness
Spiritual
Moral
Educational
Technological
Political
Economic
Social
Cultural
Psychological/Personal
-------------------**BRAIN** -------------------
Biological
Chemical/Physical
Cosmic

The "Christmas Tree" of Evolution

> This shows the 15 level by level unfolding of evolution from its "roots" in cosmic, chemical, and biological evolution up through its "branching" beyond the brain into all levels and activities characterizing the marvelous range of *human evolution*, with the *action* of each one of us vital in determining whether we move forward or backward.

In other words, one starts with the vast explosion of matter and energy into stars and planets that began it all, which constitutes the study of cosmic evolution, and from there we move upward level by level and activity by activity as the rest of it unfolds.

Level by level up the order for their emergence, we see the fifteen levels and activities for evolution prior research has identified, which became the fifteen indicators and potential major intervention points for global healing in the development of The Global Sounding.

Moving from bottom to top, we see the level by level unfolding of the "tree" of evolution from its "roots" in cosmic, chemical, and biological evolution up through its branching beyond the brain into all the levels and activities that characterize the marvelous range of human evolution that both Darwin and earlier and later thinkers visualized.

Here, in particular, two things of fundamental importance in the development of both the full spectrum theory and the Global Sounding should be noted.

One is the fact of the massive imbalance in the understanding of evolution that radically undermines social, economic, political, scientific, educational, and religious policy, thereby making effective action in the present and planning for the future very difficult and in many cases impossible.

In other words, below the pivotal placement of the brain in evolution—for *all* organisms, including ourselves—can be seen the three prior foundational levels in which at the human level science, education, and industry so far have been overwhelmingly invested: the physics, chemistry, and biology of cosmic, chemical, and biological evolution.

This is what is still primarily taught and filed in the minds of most of us as what is involved in, and of over-riding importance, whenever one hears the word evolution.

But out of the evolutionary emergence of the brain at our human level there erupts the vast variety of the eleven "higher" levels and activities of the evolutionary superstructure generally collapsed within and only cursorily dealt with as "cultural evolution."

Though the fields that explore them have been developed—for example, psychology, education, technology—still almost nowhere has there yet been any impactful investment in relating them either in theory or in practice to the primary force shaping the past, present, and future of our species and this planet: that is, to the fundamental thrust through space and time of evolution.[8]

Of particular significance to the perspective probed in *The Evolutionary Outrider,* given concrete shape and drive in *The Great Adventure*, and now operationalized in *Measuring Evolution*, is Action.

Placed here at the top, this single word Action signifies, or has been chosen to convey, the *moral* imperative of the *action* of each one of us.

It is the fact of existence on this planet that by ourselves, or within groups, determines whether we are checked, move backward, or move ahead individually and as a species.

Identifying the Indicators for the Global Sounding

Given this background, the question for scientific R&D is this:

Can applying the research and perspective of evolutionary systems science to these fifteen levels and activities be used to somehow construct a measure capable of giving us reasonably accurate reports on present and prospective future states of global health and well-being?

That is, can we, in effect—as if our world were a child, or ourselves greatly troubled by a recurring and even potentially fatal illness—construct some new kind of useful global "thermometer?"

MEASURING EVOLUTION

At first this seemed an impossible task.

In order to explore the relation of the fifteen levels and activities of evolution to the bewildering onslaught of current policies across many fields one must first define the indicators of evolutionary progress for all fifteen levels and activities.

In all practicality, anything approaching consensus among scientists and other scholars on some of these indicators is still a long way from settlement. Indeed, in view of the past history of how long it takes, it would be no exaggeration to say that proceeding as usual we would be lucky for scientists to reach consensus within another millennia. Yet in face of the evolutionary urgency, somehow this must be done—and quickly.

Should this be achieved, one must then for each of the fifteen levels and activities look for what *blocks* evolutionary progress—or the indicators for what *regresses* us, about which even less consensus presently exists among scientists and other scholars.

Finally, out of the mounting bewilderment of active governmental, social, business, religious, and other policies—which govern what happens or does not happen to all forms of life on this planet, with purportedly progressive purposes so often (as currently evident) masking underlying regressive purposes—one must also design the needed new instrument to differentiate "truth" from "lies."

Fortunately, as social scientists with the necessary training in this area of expertise and experienced test developers are aware, a huge body of work bearing on many of these difficulties has accumulated over the past century.

It fills large sections of libraries in many universities, in federal agencies such as the National Institute of Mental Health and the U.S.

Department of Education, and at Educational Testing Service in Princeton, where I was on staff while gaining my doctorate prior to my years in developing many original measures for research projects.

You can gain a sense of the extent of the prior investment of funds and expertise in this direction in our Brief, Informal History of Measures of Global Well-Being in the End Documents. Added with the needs of students and teachers as well as scientists particularly in mind, it provides a quick sketch of the pioneering work of social scientists, futurists, the Quality of Life movement, psychiatric measures, and the human potentials movement currently animated by positive psychology.

This End Document was primarily added, however, to provide a sense of the prior work I've drawn on in developing the Global Sounding. This is a vital consideration for both the expert and the decision-maker subjecting new measures to the gauntlet of determining whether or not to bless their use.

With this practical requirement in mind, it's vital to know this about measurement in science. Creativity in science generally involves extended experience in the area in question, of which I've certainly had plenty in this case. Out of this experience one then resonates to the generally large and diverse body of studies by others that shape and bolster one's own venture, which I provide here within the text and End Documents.

One files them in memory. Thereby one absorbs key names and essences into one's unconscious or preconscious mind. It is then out of one's unconscious—as happened with me and with all test-developers I know of—that in response to a specific need or target can roll the idea and shape for the sought-for measure or other solution.

One may have all the rest of this process lined up and ready to go,

MEASURING EVOLUTION

but still go nowhere without the specific spark that, so to speak, fires the engine of creativity. This is the call, or slap, or shove of the specific need or target.

In the case of the Global Sounding this call, slap and shove was the concern I share with thousands—indeed, with mounting hundreds of thousands—of scientists all over the world about what happened to America, and to the loss of sensible and inspiring American leadership to the rest of the world, during the critical opening years of the 21st century.

Transcending and yet inescapably linked to politics, this situation underlines the urgent need for the new understanding of evolution being outlined here and the development of the relatively simple matrix for the Global Sounding we'll now examine not in abstraction, as customary, but within the pressing context of the need for action.

THREE PILOT TEST OF THE POTENTIAL GLOBAL EFFECTS OF REGRESSIVE AMERICAN POLICIES

An important precursor for development of the Global Sounding was the Minnesota Multiphasic Personality Inventory.[9] Generally known as the MMPI, this is a test widely used by therapists and in personnel management for measuring degrees of personal and social maladjustments. This it does in terms of "indicators" such as ego inflation, hypomanic activation, bizarre mentation, interpersonal suspiciousness, amorality, and similar "scales."

In a comparable way, I designed the Global Sounding to use the fifteen levels and activities of evolution as "scales" for monitoring potentially positive or negative impacts of policies, projects, movements, or beliefs on global health and well-being.

Because of the well documented fact of the enormous impact of U.S. governmental, corporate, and financial policies on the "health and wealth of nations"—i.e., the economies and quality of life in all other nations—the logical pilot test for the Global Sounding was of the impact on our world of the inaugural policies for the 21st century pursued by the Bush administration and a congressional majority with heavy multinational corporate and religious backing in the United States.

MEASURING EVOLUTION

On the next page you'll find the multi-level basic matrix for the Global Sounding with positive and negative indicators and pilot test results.

Reading down along the extreme left column are the fifteen dimensions or "scales" for the Global Sounding.

These provide readings on fifteen measurable levels and activities of evolution. In each case, documentation can be found in *The Great Adventure, The Evolutionary Outrider,* in books covering thousands of studies in their notes and references, in the Library and Book Store for The Darwin Project (www.thedarwinproject.com), and here in A Brief History of the General Evolution Research Group in the End Documents.

Reading across the top, in the next two columns, are, first, "Indicators of Progression," then "Indicators of Regression." These indicators were identified by applying the perspective of evolutionary systems science to the fifteen "scales" to select indicators of evolutionary progression and regression.

For reasons explained here earlier, some of our selections will be questioned. It seems to us, however, that a majority of open-minded scientists and scholars will likely agree this is a reasonably valid set of intervening heuristics—that is, the kind of mindful "stepping stones" one needs to move in useful directions.

Again based on applying the perspectives of evolutionary systems science and progressive science to the vast number of news stories and books reporting and analyzing Bush administration and congressional policies, the final column provides a Global Sounding rating for the impact of key policies pursued by the American government during the Bush years.[10]

DAVID LOYE

The Healing of the Nations: A Global Sounding

Levels of evolution	Indicators of progression	Indicators of regression	Regressive syndrome policies
Cosmic	Sustainability of complex life forms	Environmental devastation	Opposition to environmental action and global concern
Chemical	Gaia Hypothesis/ symbiosis	Environmental devastation	Opposition to environmental action and global concern
Biological	Health and Longevity	Environmental devastation	Opposition to environmental action and global concern
BRAIN	**Parental love and nutrition**	**Lack of love and nutrition**	**Minimize governmental support**
Psychological	Self-actualizing	Lack of fulfillment	Maximize defense, minimize growth
[Cultural]	High priority for arts	Low priority for arts	Minimize support for arts
Social	Freedom and equality	Control and inequality	Maximize control and inequality

MEASURING EVOLUTION

Levels of evolution	Indicators of progression	Indicators of regression	Regressive syndrome policies
Economic	Balanced private/public	Imbalanced private/public	Maximize imbalance thru privatization
Political	Democracy	Authoritarianism	Oligarchic probe toward authoritarianism
Educational	Capacity for learning and independent thinking	Curtailing of facilities for learning and independent thinking	Radical de-escalation for progressive education
Technological	Emphasis on technologies of actualization	Emphasis on technologies of destruction	Radical escalation for the military
Moral	Living by the Golden Rule	Power of greed and corruption	Living by the Brass Rule
Spiritual	Sense of identity with humanity and greater being	Slavery to materiality	Celebration of absolute power of wealth
Consciousness	Cognitive, affective, and conative scope	Curtailing of scope of mind	Devaluing scope of mind
ACTION	Encouragement of progressive social action	Repression of progressive social action	Encouragement of *regressive* social action

© 2006 David Loye

DAVID LOYE

Summary of Pilot Test Results of the Potential Global Impact of Regressive American Policies

A crucial aspect for the development of all scientific measures is the selection of a good example of what it will be applied to in order to see if it will begin to meet the basic criteria of validity and reliability.

From "opposition to environmental action and global concern" to "encouragement of regressive social action" the results for this pilot test for the Global Sounding of American Regression Machine policies are obviously shocking. For those attuned to evolutionary advance rather than to the status quo or regression, they are also quite clear.

Those attuned to advance will likely find that in this evidence that regressive American policies threaten to drive our species backward on *all fifteen* levels and activities for evolution reasonable proof of what is known as *construct* validity for the Global Sounding.

As for those attuned to the status quo, the Global Sounding and these pilot test results will be written off as "unfairly biased," "questionably grounded," or constitute a case for the poking and prodding and saying maybe yes, maybe no that can endlessly delay putting new measures to an effectively wide use.

The classic case here is that of French psychologist Alfred Binet's development of the original IQ test, which year after year failed to gain acceptance in France until American psychologists took it over to develop the pioneering, and now universally in use, Stanford-Binet IQ.[11]

For the regressives, of course, nothing but the howling of anathema and the hurling of brickbats at the Global Sounding will serve the cause.

MEASURING EVOLUTION

For skeptics and all the rest of us to note, however, is this "new" fact about evolution, which advanced work in practically all fields of science today is finding.

For over 100 years the popular prevailing impression has been that evolution takes place very slowly—if not over aeons then at the very least many centuries. But the consistent finding for the work upon which chaos theory and all other so-called nonlinear theories are based is that *under the right circumstances* evolution can take place *extraordinarily fast*—within seconds to weeks or months depending on the level and activity.[12]

Along with traditional findings, it is this advanced work bearing on the varying speed of evolution for all fifteen levels and activities for science upon which development of the Global Sounding measure is based.

In other words, those inclined to discount Global Sounding results should ponder the fact that the alignment of its fifteen scales to the extensive scientific grounding for the fifteen levels and activities for evolution reflects advanced findings for the fields of physics, chemistry, biology, brain science, psychology, sociology, economics, political science, education, and the sciences of morality, spirituality, consciousness, and action—or the thrust of "conscious evolution."

And the most important thing about all of this is this fact still almost wholly unrealized outside the understanding of still only a tiny fraction of scientists.

The frightening fact that makes understanding and action in this regard so urgent is the speed with which rapid change can happen *in either a progressive or regressive direction.*

The evidence is not only of how rapid evolution can take place in a progressive or life-favoring direction. Hauntingly echoing current concern about global warming on the environmental level is the consistent finding on the social level of how—as in the case of the swift rise and impact of the Nazis in Germany on the levels of political and moral evolution—evolution can shift in a regressive, life-diminishing, or *de*volutionary direction.

In other words, the fears internationally of scholars in many fields regarding what is happening in America are not exaggerations, but grimly and factually supported by a rock solid scientific grounding.

To adequately dramatize this vital factor within the context of our concern with use of the Global Sounding to regularly measure and help advance and maintain global well-being, we've included the Lovelock Statement of Global Urgency among our End Documents.

This aspect alone should be sufficient reason calling for the mobilizing of a new across-the-board alliance of progressive money, science, education, politics, and morality and spirituality.

FOUR HOW TO USE IT *I*:
 THE GLOBAL SOUNDING MEASURE WITH BASIC
 MATRIX AND BLANK FORMS FOR ITS USE BY PEOPLE
 IN BUSINESS, GOVERNMENT, POLITICS, SCIENCE,
 EDUCATION, WRITERS, THE MEDIA, NONPROFIT AND
 RELIGIOUS ORGANIZATIONS, AND PHILANTHROPISTS
 AND FOUNDATIONS

In providing a reading on where we seem to be today in terms of the ups and downs of 100,000 years of human evolution, the Global Sounding is designed to be used as a guide to the investment of time and money in all of the above and other situations of many kinds and sizes in our lives today.

All you have to do is focus on whatever cause, project, or policies you are considering putting time and/or money into.

Then follow these steps using the following handy form.

1. Write down cause, project, or policy in the bracketed blank at the top.

2. With this subject in mind, scan down through the Indicators of Progression (+) and the Indicators of Regression (-).

3. For each level or activity of evolution (first column), ask yourself whether by investing time or money into the proposal for testing (your entry in the blank at top) you are likely to influence evolutionary *progression* (second column).

Or evolutionary *regression* (third column).

Or neither.

Or the question at this level or activity for evolution is just not relevant in your case.

4. If it seems the proposal might influence evolutionary *progression*, in the fourth column enter a plus (+ 1) in the blank.

5. If it seems it might influence evolutionary *regression*, in the fourth column enter a minus (– 1) in the blank.

6. If it is hard to guess whether it would be of influence either way, or otherwise seems irrelevant, enter zero (0) in the blank.

7. At the end, add up your pluses, minuses, and zeros, and enter the result in the blank for the Global Sounding Total.

To get the "feel" for use of this measure, refer to the example of the pilot test for Regressive American Policies shown earlier, or to the wide range of hypothetical examples that follow here in the next chapter.

If you find other wordings for either Indicators of Progression or Regression that seem to better fit the proposal you're testing, change the wording to fit your situation—and let us know of your change and why.

All measures until fully perfected are works in progress. By sharing your experience in using the Global Sounding you can help guarantee the end project is as nearly close to universal applicability as possible.

For this reason, please send copies of all successful—as well as unsuccessful—uses of this new measure to loye@benjaminfranklinpress.com.

This caution, however. Further development of this measure by others for commercial purposes is outlawed by our copyright including

MEASURING EVOLUTION

work underway on a computerized version.

When ready, we will consider partnerships with established test developing and marketing companies. In the meantime, however, our copyright and considerable prior investment must be respected.

DAVID LOYE

Blank Form for Universal Use

A Global Sounding of the Impact of

[[_____]]

Levels of evolution	Indicators of progression (+)	Indicators of regression (-)	Enter impact (+, -, 0)
Cosmic	Sustainability of complex life forms	Environmental devastation	_____
Chemical	Gaia hypothesis/ symbiosis	Environmental devastation	_____
Biological	Health and longevity	Environmental devastation	_____
BRAIN	Parental love and nutrition	Lack of love and nutrition	_____
Psychological	Self-actualizing	Lack of fulfillment	_____
[Cultural]	High priority for arts	Low priority for arts	_____
Social	Freedom and equality	Control and inequality	_____

MEASURING EVOLUTION

Levels of evolution	Indicators of progression (+)	Indicators of regression (-)	Enter impact (+, -, 0)
Economic	Balanced private/public	Imbalanced private/public	_____
Political	Democracy	Authoritarianism	_____
Educational	Capacity for learning and independent thinking	Curtailing of facilities for learning and independent thinking	_____
Technological	Emphasis on technologies of actualization	Emphasis on technologies of destruction	_____
Moral	Living by the Golden Rule	Power of greed and corruption	_____
Spiritual	Sense of identity with humanity and greater being	Slavery to materiality	_____
Consciousness	Cognitive, affective, and conative scope	Curtailing of scope of mind	_____
ACTION	Encouragement of progressive social action	Repression of progressive social action	_____
	GLOBAL SOUNDING TOTAL		_____

© David Loye 2006

FIVE   HOW TO USE IT *II* :
EXAMPLES FOR USE BY PEOPLE IN BUSINESS, GOVERNMENT, POLITICS, SCIENCE, EDUCATION, WRITERS, THE MEDIA, NONPROFIT AND RELIGIOUS ORGANIZATIONS, AND PHILANTHROPISTS AND FOUNDATIONS

To facilitate use of the Global Sounding this chapter provides examples of hypothetical proposals and situations for people in business, government, politics, science, education, nonprofit and religious organizations, and philanthropists and foundations.

In each case we first sketch the task or *goal* for a specific proposal.

Then we sketch the hypothetical *situation* that decision-makers might face in terms of the opposing views within a decision-making group—or within yourself—of differing ways of carrying out the task or reaching the proposed goal.

Let us say, for example, that you are a responsible decision-maker in a hypothetical situation in business, government, a foundation, politics, et cetera.

You are a manager or leader, who must by yourself decide on the right course to take.

Or you are a member of a key management group, or board, or council, who must decide in counsel with others.

Your task is first to listen to—and privately evaluate—all

supporting and opposing views.

If the debate is within yourself, by yourself, the decision of course is up to you, sink or swim.

If you're in a group, however, customarily the more venturesome will state their observations and conclusions. Then the rest will follow in a more or less unconscious process of taking sides.

Thinking upon your own experience in such situations, consider how often you have seen decisions in such situations reached not according to what seems most sensible to the most knowledgeable and well-qualified to reach the right decision.

Think of all the times you have seen decisions reached solely according to hidden agendas, old loyalties, or just a wild guess.

With the explosive development of technologies capable of devastating huge areas within a few short years, or destroying millions of us within seconds, no other time in world history has had so much riding on this customary situation—private, arbitrary, unmonitored, restricted only by conscience and fear of the law—for both individual and group decision-making in government, business, politics, economics, and every other institution of planetary impact.

What the Global Sounding is designed to provide in this situation is a new measure for shoring up intelligence and protecting yourself and others from possible disaster. Its blank forms are specifically designed to put the decisions you must reach within the larger context that increasingly affects everything these days.

Global warming, strip mining, clear-cutting forests, polluting of the air, water, and land are a few of numerous environmental examples where the blind greed of the few guts the quality and even endangers the lives of all the rest of us. The advantage for the Global Sounding is that in the following hypothetical examples you can see how beyond such familiar examples this simple blank form can cover a surprising spread for the critical spectrum for evaluations.

A further advantage is that the Global Sounding matrix and blank form provides a useful exercise for gaining—potentially within remarkably few minutes—decisions aligned with *positive* or progressive evolution. This, rather than routine alignment with the seemingly safe but often deceptive status quo – or blind or blinded advocacy for regression.

In the examples that follow here, we provide blank forms as they might be filled out by the decision-makers involved—for, against, or uncertain about proposals.

In each case, we then close with a sketch of a sample scenario for the new measure's successful use.

Real life situations for you will of course usually be more complex and cloudy. But at times you may find our pitting of extremes against one another, as well as other nuances of the decision-making process, usefully mirrors what's happening today.

In any case, these examples illustrate how to use the Global Sounding and blank forms to gain better decisions for yourself, your organization, and the rest of us trying to live in peace, with hope for some reasonable degree of security and prosperity in this world.

Again, your experience with this new measure can be invaluable to others. Please send brief reports of all successful—and unsuccessful—uses of this new measure to loye@benjaminfranklinpress.com.

BUSINESS

Proposal: Location of a new manufacturing plant for Amalgamated Amalgamite, Inc.

Situation: A decision must be reached between location in Country X versus Country Y.

Country X has no environmental laws and lower wages but potentially higher corporate profitability. Country Y has environmental laws and somewhat higher wages but offers potentially lower corporate profitability.

Advocates for environmentally-sensitive Country Y claim greater social stability for Country Y and gains in positive corporate global image will offset lower profits.

Advocates for environmentally-insensitive Country X claim this is exaggerated—and privately stress that whether or not this is true, what matters in terms of corporate management survival is the bottom line for the quarterly report for earnings and effect on the stock market.

For some initial grounding for the ensuing discussion, all present are asked to use Global Sounding blank forms to rate both prospects.

On comparing the two rating forms, advocates for Country X immediately refuse to fill them out. But intimidating them by insisting "Fair is fair," advocates for Country Y fill out both forms.

Composite results (for calculating, see Note eight[13]) for the advocates follow. First for Country X. Then for Country Y.

DAVID LOYE

A GLOBAL SOUNDING OF THE IMPACT OF

[[*Construction of a New Manufacturing Plant for Our Company in Country X*]]

Levels of evolution	Indicators of progression (+)	Indicators of regression (-)	Enter impact (+, -, 0)
Cosmic	Sustainability of complex life forms	Environmental devastation	____-1____
Chemical	Gaia hypothesis/ symbiosis	Environmental devastation	____-1____
Biological	Health and longevity	Environmental devastation	____-1____
BRAIN	**Parental love and nutrition**	**Lack of love and nutrition**	____-1____
Psychological	Self-actualizing	Lack of fulfillment	____-1____
[Cultural]	High priority for arts	Low priority for arts	____-1____
Social	Freedom and equality	Control and inequality	____-1____

MEASURING EVOLUTION

Levels of evolution	Indicators of progression (+)	Indicators of regression (-)	Enter impact (+, -, 0)
Economic	Balanced private/public	Imbalanced private/public	0
Political	Democracy	Authoritarianism	0
Educational	Capacity for learning and independent thinking	Curtailing of facilities for learning and independent thinking	-1
Technological	Emphasis on technologies of actualization	Emphasis on technologies of destruction	0
Moral	Living by the Golden Rule	Power of greed and corruption	-1
Spiritual	Sense of identity with humanity and greater being	Slavery to materiality	-1
Consciousness	Cognitive, affective, and conative scope	Curtailing of scope of mind	-1
ACTION	Encouragement of progressive social action	Repression of progressive social action	0
	GLOBAL SOUNDING TOTAL		-11

© David Loye 2006

DAVID LOYE

A GLOBAL SOUNDING OF THE IMPACT OF

[[*Construction of a New Manufacturing Plant for Our Company in Country Y*]]

Levels of evolution	Indicators of progression (+)	Indicators of regression (-)	Enter impact (+, -, 0)
Cosmic	Sustainability of complex life forms	Environmental devastation	_____1_____
Chemical	Gaia hypothesis/ symbiosis	Environmental devastation	_____1_____
Biological	Health and longevity	Environmental devastation	_____1_____
BRAIN	**Parental love and nutrition**	**Lack of love and nutrition**	_____1_____
Psychological	Self-actualizing	Lack of fulfillment	_____1_____
[Cultural]	High priority for arts	Low priority for arts	_____0_____
Social	Freedom and equality	Control and inequality	_____0_____

MEASURING EVOLUTION

Levels of evolution	Indicators of progression (+)	Indicators of regression (-)	Enter impact (+, -, 0)
Economic	Balanced private/public	Imbalanced private/public	_____0_____
Political	Democracy	Authoritarianism	_____0_____
Educational	Capacity for learning and independent thinking	Curtailing of facilities for learning and independent thinking	_____1_____
Technological	Emphasis on technologies of actualization	Emphasis on technologies of destruction	_____1_____
Moral	Living by the Golden Rule	Power of greed and corruption	_____1_____
Spiritual	Sense of identity with humanity and greater being	Slavery to materiality	_____1_____
Consciousness	Cognitive, affective, and conative scope	Curtailing of scope of mind	_____1_____
ACTION	Encouragement of progressive social action	Repression of progressive social action	_____0_____
	GLOBAL SOUNDING TOTAL		_____10_____

© David Loye 2006

DAVID LOYE

Strategies and Scenarios for Success

Comparison of Global Sounding results: For Country X, – 11. For Country Y, + 10.

Scenario: Within companies, in all except the most autocratic, decisions are reached through the arguments and politics pro and con of advocates of various positions against one another.

In this example the Global Sounding is—and in most comparable examples will be—used by progressives in arguments to focus attention on factors that otherwise will be ignored, neglected, or steam-rollered.

The goal is to win swing votes against the customary imbalance in power favoring defenders of the status quo and regressives.

In this example for Amalgamated Amalgamites, on processing and presentation of results, advocates for Country X and the status quo immediately charged that this was unfair as it was just "guesswork" on the part of the progressives and others upon whom the progressives had forced this questionable process.

Progressive advocates for Country Y came back with the fact the measure is based on at the very least two decades of research involved hundreds of scientists on factors advancing or undermining or driving back human evolution.

"What kind of future do you want for your children and grandchildren?" they asked.

"What do you want our company—and yourselves—to be known for?"

MEASURING EVOLUTION

" What kind of image are we trying to build with all the money going into PR and advertising?"

(A device for strengthening the progressive case at minimal cost is to distribute copies of *The Great Adventure: Toward a Fully Human Theory of Evolution* (State University Press of New York, 2004) and/or *Measuring Evolution* (Benjamin Franklin Press, 2006), as one or two of many examples of the heavy-weight scientific backing for serious consideration of Global Sounding results for Amalgamated Amalgamites).

As the discussion went on—in contrast to the cold presentation of statistics cocked to show nothing but the so-called "bottom line" shorn of all the wider ramifications—the progressives adroitly kept focusing and refocusing on points raised in their favor by the Global Sounding.

End results: By the hairline but decisive difference of a vote of six to five—against previous expectations—the progressives won and the company's new manufacturing plant was built in the environmentally sensitive and somewhat higher wage Country Y instead of "bottom of the barrel" Country X.

GOVERNMENT

Proposal: Funding a Missile Defense System.

Situation: A decision must be reached between investment in an increase for a missile defense system or an expansion for the Head Start program to give disadvantaged pre-schoolers a better chance in life.

Advocates for the Missile Defense System privately and publicly very effectively pound the drum for it by raising the spectre of the decimation of American cities by enemy missiles otherwise. Privately, among the "inner circle," they note the immense political advantages to be gained by shifting more billions to the companies of the military-industrial complex in return for more millions back in campaign contributions.

Advocates for the Head Start Program both privately and publicly call attention to the overwhelming number of scientists who decry the Missile Defense System as an ineffective boondoggle for the greed of tunnel-visioned companies and politicians. They also point to page after page of cost-to-benefit statistics showing the immense national gains for the Head Start investment.

The key decision—which will most decisively affect the way it will go on other levels of government—is to be reached in a Senate committee heavily loaded with members with either defense

MEASURING EVOLUTION

industries or military bases in their states. To make the situation even more difficult, the Chairman has set the meeting for a date, time, and very small room designed to discourage attendance or press coverage.

Senatorial Head Start advocates counter with an announcement to the press of "an historic and innovative first use of the new Global Sounding measure to help streamline determination of governmental priorities."

Before the newsmen and television cameras crammed into the tiny room, Head Start program advocates distribute the Global Sounding forms to all present – both Missile Defense System as well as Head Start Program advocates, and of course the press.

Missile Defense System advocates refuse to touch the forms. Head Start Program advocates then distribute the following composite result for their evaluation to all present.

DAVID LOYE

A GLOBAL SOUNDING OF THE IMPACT OF

[[Funding a Missile Defense System]]

Levels of evolution	Indicators of progression (+)	Indicators of regression (-)	Enter impact (+, -, 0)
Cosmic	Sustainability of complex life forms	Environmental devastation	____-1____
Chemical	Gaia hypothesis/ symbiosis	Environmental devastation	____-1____
Biological	Health and longevity	Environmental devastation	____-1____
BRAIN	**Parental love and nutrition**	**Lack of love and nutrition**	____-1____
Psychological	Self-actualizing	Lack of fulfillment	____-1____
[Cultural]	High priority for arts	Low priority for arts	____-1____
Social	Freedom and equality	Control and inequality	____-1____

MEASURING EVOLUTION

Levels of evolution	Indicators of progression (+)	Indicators of regression (-)	Enter impact (+, -, 0)
Economic	Balanced private/public	Imbalanced private/public	0
Political	Democracy	Authoritarianism	0
Educational	Capacity for learning and independent thinking	Curtailing of facilities for learning and independent thinking	-1
Technological	Emphasis on technologies of actualization	Emphasis on technologies of destruction	-1
Moral	Living by the Golden Rule	Power of greed and corruption	-1
Spiritual	Sense of identity with humanity and greater being	Slavery to materiality	-1
Consciousness	Cognitive, affective, and conative scope	Curtailing of scope of mind	-1
ACTION	Encouragement of progressive social action	Repression of progressive social action	-1
	GLOBAL SOUNDING TOTAL		-13

© David Loye 2006

DAVID LOYE

A GLOBAL SOUNDING OF THE IMPACT OF

[[Funding Head Start Program Expansion]]

Levels of evolution	Indicators of progression (+)	Indicators of regression (-)	Enter impact (+, -, 0)
Cosmic	Sustainability of complex life forms	Environmental devastation	____1____
Chemical	Gaia hypothesis/ symbiosis	Environmental devastation	____1____
Biological	Health and longevity	Environmental devastation	____1____
BRAIN	**Parental love and nutrition**	**Lack of love and nutrition**	____1____
Psychological	Self-actualizing	Lack of fulfillment	____1____
[Cultural]	High priority for arts	Low priority for arts	____1____
Social	Freedom and equality	Control and inequality	____1____

MEASURING EVOLUTION

Levels of evolution	Indicators of progression (+)	Indicators of regression (-)	Enter impact (+, -, 0)
Economic	Balanced private/public	Imbalanced private/public	1
Political	Democracy	Authoritarianism	1
Educational	Capacity for learning and independent thinking	Curtailing of facilities for learning and independent thinking	1
Technological	Emphasis on technologies of actualization	Emphasis on technologies of destruction	1
Moral	Living by the Golden Rule	Power of greed and corruption	1
Spiritual	Sense of identity with humanity and greater being	Slavery to materiality	1
Consciousness	Cognitive, affective, and conative scope	Curtailing of scope of mind	1
ACTION	Encouragement of progressive social action	Repression of progressive social action	1
	GLOBAL SOUNDING TOTAL		15

© David Loye 2006

DAVID LOYE

Strategies and Scenarios for Success

Comparison of Global Sounding results: For Missile System Funding, – 13. For Head Start Program Expansion, + 15.

Scenario: The strategy is based on the fact that within governments, in all except the most autocratic, decisions are reached through the arguments and politics pro and con of advocates of various positions against one another.

In this example the Global Sounding is—and in most comparable examples will be—used by progressives in arguments to focus attention on factors that otherwise will be ignored or neglected in contention to win swing votes against the customary imbalance in power favoring defenders of the status quo and regressives.

In this example, on presentation of both results by the progressives through distribution of neat copies with color highlights to both committee members and press, the status quo charged this was unfair as well as ridiculous.

"It's just guesswork," they charged. "A biased sample," another said. "Airy fairy dressed up to look like science," another claimed.

Progressives came back with the fact the measure is based on at least two decades of research involved hundreds of scientists on factors advancing or undermining or driving back human evolution.

"What kind of future do you want for your children and grandchildren?" they charged back – with obvious pick up by the cameras and the notepads for the press. "What do you want your Party—and yourselves—to be known for?"

(Again, a good device for strengthening this case at minimal cost

MEASURING EVOLUTION

is to distribute copies of *The Great Adventure: Toward a Fully Human Theory of Evolution* (State University Press of New York, 2004), and/or *Measuring Evolution: A User's Guide to the Health and Wealth of Nation,* as examples of the heavy-weight scientific backing for use and serious consideration by all of Global Sounding results).

For a while the battle raged between Missile System advocates with pictures of mushroom clouds and decimated cities and Head Start advocates with pictures of gamboling healthy children, both accompanied with big charts of statistics. But again and again progressives kept adroitly focusing and refocusing on points raised in their favor by the Global Sounding.

End results: By a vote of seven to six—and in face of secret promises of ten millions in campaign contributions and golfing for all in Scotland to Missile System advocates—the progressives won. And the children of Head Start got the funding instead of the lobbyists, executives, stockholders, and political supporters for big defense contractors in California and Georgia.

POLITICS

Proposal: Put $400,000 into negative campaign ads and an undercover "dirty tricks" rumor mill against opponent.

Situation: A decision must be reached by Dudley Doright and staff and advisors on where best to invest money for his campaign against Tess Trueheart for the U.S. House of Representatives.

Doright and Trueheart have been running neck and neck in the polls, but with mounting endorsements for Trueheart by the League of Women Voters, NOW, ACLU, the Sierra Club, etc., etc., the polls are now shifting to Trueheart's favor. Without something new and dramatic to seize public attention, it looks like Doright will lose.

Advocates for negative ads and dirty tricks point to the undeniable success of this strategy in gaining and retaining the presidency for both U.S. presidents Richard Nixon and George W. Bush. They also point to the highly skilled corps for doing this kept at the ready retained in various good positions in the favored American industries backing Doright.

Advocates for putting the money into positive ads are trying to make the case for an ethical campaign. They point to a groundswell of public opinion turning against such tactics and the success of this strategy elsewhere in the world. They also point to the rise of a new generation of muckrakers in print as well as internet media out for blood in the case of dirty tricks and similar underhanded tactics.

MEASURING EVOLUTION

To bolster their case for sticking to higher ground they turn to use of the new Global Sounding measure. Dirty tricks advocates refuse to touch the forms, but Doright and key advisors agree to carefully consider the composite results for higher ground advocates.

DAVID LOYE

A GLOBAL SOUNDING OF THE IMPACT OF

[[$400,000 to Negative Campaign Ads and Dirty Tricks]]

Levels of evolution	Indicators of progression (+)	Indicators of regression (-)	Enter impact (+, -, 0)
Cosmic	Sustainability of complex life forms	Environmental devastation	0
Chemical	Gaia hypothesis/ symbiosis	Environmental devastation	0
Biological	Health and longevity	Environmental devastation	0
BRAIN	Parental love and nutrition	Lack of love and nutrition	-1
Psychological	Self-actualizing	Lack of fulfillment	-1
[Cultural]	High priority for arts	Low priority for arts	0
Social	Freedom and equality	Control and inequality	-1

MEASURING EVOLUTION

Levels of evolution	Indicators of progression (+)	Indicators of regression (-)	Enter impact (+, -, 0)
Economic	Balanced private/public	Imbalanced private/public	0
Political	Democracy	Authoritarianism	-1
Educational	Capacity for learning and independent thinking	Curtailing of facilities for learning and independent thinking	-1
Technological	Emphasis on technologies of actualization	Emphasis on technologies of destruction	0
Moral	Living by the Golden Rule	Power of greed and corruption	-1
Spiritual	Sense of identity with humanity and greater being	Slavery to materiality	-1
Consciousness	Cognitive, affective, and conative scope	Curtailing of scope of mind	-1
ACTION	Encouragement of progressive social action	Repression of progressive social action	-1
	GLOBAL SOUNDING TOTAL		-9

© David Loye 2006

DAVID LOYE

A GLOBAL SOUNDING OF THE IMPACT OF

[[$400,000 to Positive Campaign Ads and no Dirty Tricks]]

Levels of evolution	Indicators of progression (+)	Indicators of regression (-)	Enter impact (+, -, 0)
Cosmic	Sustainability of complex life forms	Environmental devastation	0
Chemical	Gaia hypothesis/ symbiosis	Environmental devastation	0
Biological	Health and longevity	Environmental devastation	0
BRAIN	**Parental love and nutrition**	**Lack of love and nutrition**	0
Psychological	Self-actualizing	Lack of fulfillment	1
[Cultural]	High priority for arts	Low priority for arts	0
Social	Freedom and equality	Control and inequality	1

MEASURING EVOLUTION

Levels of evolution	Indicators of progression (+)	Indicators of regression (-)	Enter impact (+, -, 0)
Economic	Balanced private/public	Imbalanced private/public	0
Political	Democracy	Authoritarianism	1
Educational	Capacity for learning and independent thinking	Curtailing of facilities for learning and independent thinking	1
Technological	Emphasis on technologies of actualization	Emphasis on technologies of destruction	1
Moral	Living by the Golden Rule	Power of greed and corruption	1
Spiritual	Sense of identity with humanity and greater being	Slavery to materiality	1
Consciousness	Cognitive, affective, and conative scope	Curtailing of scope of mind	1
ACTION	Encouragement of progressive social action	Repression of progressive social action	1
	GLOBAL SOUNDING TOTAL		9

© David Loye 2006

DAVID LOYE

Strategies and Scenarios for Success

Comparison of Global Sounding results: For Negative Ads and Dirty Tricks, − 9. For Positive Ads and No Dirty Tricks, + 9.

Scenario: As viewers of "West Wing" and (all too briefly) "Commander in Chief" on American television have become aware, within political campaigns all decisions are reached through the arguments and politics pro and con of advocates of various positions contending with one another.

In this example the Global Sounding is—and in most comparable examples will be—used by progressives in arguments to focus attention on factors that otherwise will be ignored or neglected in contention to win swing votes against the customary imbalance in power favoring defenders of the status quo and regressives.

In this example, in the meeting for the key decision, to Doright, staff, and advisors, progressives distributed neat copies with color highlights for their evaluations of dirty tricks versus positive ads.

Negative ad advocates were actually—or at least pretended to be—supportive.

"Look, this is all very well and good. We agree this is the kind of ad we'd like to keep running. But the cold, hard fact is that by putting money into ads emphasizing Doright alignment with some of these noble purposes you're going to cut off crucial big money from key backers. You're also going to lose the vote of all the schmucks hankering for dirt that can tip the election our way. Win with the schmucks or lose with the mensch—that's our choice."

MEASURING EVOLUTION

Progressives came back with the fact that the Global Sounding is based on at least two decades of research involving hundreds of scientists on factors advancing or undermining and driving back human evolution.

"We'll concede that's going to cut no ice with important segments we're going for. But the main thing is this. The Moral Code based on this Global Sounding. By aligning us with the Global Sounding Moral Code points for agreement between liberals and conservatives, we can stir up churches of both varieties in our favor. Tess is just hooked into the standard liberal set with nothing going for her openly by the churches. Put the money into ads – and contacts – aimed at getting the churches on our side, and out in force, and we can still tip things in our favor."

(Again, a device for strengthening this case at minimal cost would be to distribute copies of *Measuring Evolution* with the section tabbed for the Global Sounding Moral Code. Also in cases of this sort, the visual reminder of pictures of Richard Nixon and George W. Bush riding high in their day versus pictures of George Washington, Abraham Lincoln, and Dwight Eisenhower could be useful).

And so it was that, while the discussion went back and forth, progressives kept adroitly focusing and refocusing on points raised in their favor by the Global Sounding.

End results: By a vote of eleven to ten—and in face of the promise of the free services of a disciple of chief Bushite henchman Karl Rove "just for the fun of it"—the progressives won and fair fight tactics prevailed over dirty tricks for the campaign.

SCIENCE

Proposal: Expand research and curricula in social and systems scientific studies of progression versus regression in human evolution.

Situation: A decision must be reached by the prestigious Maynard Elliot University on an allocation of a gift of $400,000 to the University for expenditure to its Department of Graduate Studies. The donor has expressed no preference other than: "I leave it to you to determine what emphasis may best serve the world at this time."

Progressives have moved speedily to propose an expansion of research and curricula in social and systems scientific studies of evolution.

They point to the need for new work in this direction revealed by the startling new humanistic reconstruction of Darwin's lost emphasis on moral sensitivity in the his theory of evolution. They argue that the reconstruction reveals a basic imbalance in the valuing and use of science, which in turn perpetuates disastrous social beliefs and policies. They note that funding their proposal will elevate Maynard Elliot University with a new global reputation as a scientific and social pioneer. They urge all involved in the decision to view the case for both research and curricula made by the Darwin Project website: www.thedarwinproject.com.

"If you sort down through all the confusion," they say, "what an unbiased systems science reveals is this. The basic problem is the entrenched heavy support for the natural sciences and the old Darwinian model of 'survival of the fittest' and 'selfishness as the prime driver,' which perpetuate a social system cocked toward war and wealth and power for the few, and minimal support for the humanistic natural, social, and systems sciences, which for over 100 years now have been battling uphill to try to gain a world of lasting peace and plenty for all."

The heads of the Physics, Chemistry, and Biology Departments—long established and heavily entrenched within the academic hierarchy—vigorously object. This, they say, is a gross, misleading, and politically tainted over-simplification. They point to the fact that it is their established drawing power for both governmental and private foundation grants that accounts for the lion's share of funding for the University. They also produce a long list of what is still needed for all three of their Departments "simply to keep up with other leaders in our basic fields."

"Is Maynard Elliot to be known for the waste of money in pursuit of radical chimera such as this so-called new Darwin thing? Is it to sink into all the confusion and controversies of the social sciences? Or is it to continue to be known for its rock firm grounding in the fundamental science of Einstein, Heisenberg, Mendel and the real Darwin?"

All graciously agree to fill in the Global Sounding forms urged by proposal advocates upon the President, Provost, and heads of all relevant Departments and advisors. Only the President, Provost, and advocates for the proposal, however, actually fill in the forms, with the following composite result.

DAVID LOYE

A GLOBAL SOUNDING OF THE IMPACT OF

[[Proposal to expand research and curricula in social and systems scientific studies of progression versus regression in human evolution]]

Levels of evolution	Indicators of progression (+)	Indicators of regression (-)	Enter impact (+, -, 0)
Cosmic	Sustainability of complex life forms	Environmental devastation	_____0_____
Chemical	Gaia hypothesis/ symbiosis	Environmental devastation	_____0_____
Biological	Health and longevity	Environmental devastation	_____0_____
BRAIN	Parental love and nutrition	Lack of love and nutrition	_____1_____
Psychological	Self-actualizing	Lack of fulfillment	_____1_____
[Cultural]	High priority for arts	Low priority for arts	_____1_____
Social	Freedom and equality	Control and inequality	_____1_____

MEASURING EVOLUTION

Levels of evolution	Indicators of progression (+)	Indicators of regression (-)	Enter impact (+, -, 0)
Economic	Balanced private/public	Imbalanced private/public	_____1_____
Political	Democracy	Authoritarianism	_____1_____
Educational	Capacity for learning and independent thinking	Curtailing of facilities for learning and independent thinking	_____1_____
Technological	Emphasis on technologies of actualization	Emphasis on technologies of destruction	_____1_____
Moral	Living by the Golden Rule	Power of greed and corruption	_____1_____
Spiritual	Sense of identity with humanity and greater being	Slavery to materiality	_____1_____
Consciousness	Cognitive, affective, and conative scope	Curtailing of scope of mind	_____1_____
ACTION	Encouragement of progressive social action	Repression of progressive social action	_____1_____
	GLOBAL SOUNDING TOTAL		_____12_____

© David Loye 2006

DAVID LOYE

A GLOBAL SOUNDING OF THE IMPACT OF

[[Alternative funding for present Physics, Chemistry, and Biology Departments]]

Levels of evolution	Indicators of progression (+)	Indicators of regression (-)	Enter impact (+, -, 0)
Cosmic	Sustainability of complex life forms	Environmental devastation	_____1_____
Chemical	Gaia hypothesis/ symbiosis	Environmental devastation	_____1_____
Biological	Health and longevity	Environmental devastation	_____1_____
BRAIN	Parental love and nutrition	Lack of love and nutrition	_____1_____
Psychological	Self-actualizing	Lack of fulfillment	_____0_____
[Cultural]	High priority for arts	Low priority for arts	_____0_____
Social	Freedom and equality	Control and inequality	_____0_____

MEASURING EVOLUTION

Levels of evolution	Indicators of progression (+)	Indicators of regression (-)	Enter impact (+, -, 0)
Economic	Balanced private/public	Imbalanced private/public	0
Political	Democracy	Authoritarianism	0
Educational	Capacity for learning and independent thinking	Curtailing of facilities for learning and independent thinking	1
Technological	Emphasis on technologies of actualization	Emphasis on technologies of destruction	0
Moral	Living by the Golden Rule	Power of greed and corruption	0
Spiritual	Sense of identity with humanity and greater being	Slavery to materiality	0
Consciousness	Cognitive, affective, and conative scope	Curtailing of scope of mind	0
ACTION	Encouragement of progressive social action	Repression of progressive social action	0
	GLOBAL SOUNDING TOTAL		5

© David Loye 2006

DAVID LOYE

Strategies and Scenarios for Success

Comparison of Global Sounding results: For Expansion in Social and Systems Science, +12. For Physics, Chemistry, and Biology Department needs, + 5.

Scenario: As everyone who, as a natural, social, or systems scientist, has lived and worked within the university and higher academic world knows, practically all decisions are reached through the arguments and politics pro and con of advocates of various positions contending with one another.

In this example the Global Sounding is—and in most comparable examples will be—used by progressives in arguments to focus attention on factors that otherwise will be ignored or neglected in contention to win swing votes against the customary imbalance in power favoring defenders of the status quo and regressives.

In this example, on presentation of their results by the progressives through distribution of neat copies with color highlights to the President, Provost, Controller, and all others gathered for the discussion and key decision, advocates for the traditional emphasis put their position this way.

"We agree that in the best of all possible worlds there would be more emphasis on the directions ostensibly supported by this highly questionable Global Sounding form. But this is *not* the best of all possible worlds. Closing in on us are a series of environmental catastrophes, and an increase in terrorism and military threats, that can only be adequately measured and met by adequate funding of the basic work of our basic fields. Our cyclotron and our laboratories are the advance guard for the nation. However, we might want to indulge ourselves into trying to create utopia on earth, we must face fact and put the money into the funding of national survival at a time of overwhelming threat."

Progressives came back with the fact the Global Sounding indicators for advancing or undermining and driving back human evolution are based not only on at least two decades of research involving thousands of social and systems scientists, but also on the work of scores of leading and Nobel prize winners in physics, chemistry, and biology.

"If those great figures in the development of physics, chemistry, and biology—if Einstein, Heisenberg, Mendel and, as you put it, the real Darwin were here—which proposal do you suppose they would support? Einstein, who deplored that his contribution of $E = MC^2$ led to the atom bomb? Heisenberg, who spent the rest of his life trying to make up for the fact he was forced to work for the Nazis? Mendel, who was a notably gentle and caring priest? And the 'real Darwin,' who in *The Descent of Man* wrote only twice of "survival of the fittest," but 95 times of love and 92 times of moral sensitivity?"

(Useful for strengthening the case at this point at minimal cost would be distribution of *The Great Adventure: Toward a Fully Human Theory of* Evolution and/or *Bankrolling Evolution,* with pages on the new facts about Darwin tabbed).

And so it was that, while the opposition displayed greater ingenuity in making their case than had ever been seen before, progressives adroitly kept focusing and refocusing on points raised in their favor by the Global Sounding.

DAVID LOYE

End results: By a vote of eleven to ten—and in face even of talk of a grant from an industrial giant to match the $400,000 if the disputed money went to Physics, Chemistry, and Biology – the progressives won and the new venture in evolutionary-oriented social and systems science prevailed.

EDUCATION

Proposal: Shift teaching of evolution in all schools in California from restriction to "first-half" Darwinism to the full Darwinian theory of evolution.

Situation: A decision must be reached by an alliance of the state Parent and Teachers Association (PTA) with the state League of Women Voters association on what policies and projects to promote with key legislators, the State Department of Education, and local school boards.

Delegations from Berkeley and Santa Cruz advocates of the proposal urge that a plank for the alliance be the push for shifting the teaching of evolution in all schools in California from the long established traditional emphasis on the "old" Darwinian to the "new" Darwinian theory and story of evolution.

They capture the attention of everybody with a power point presentation showing that in *The Descent of Man* not only did Darwin write only twice of the 100-year-old emphasis on "survival of the fittest," but 95 times of love and 92 times of moral sensitivity. In contrast also to the "new" sociobiological idea that human evolution is driven by "selfish genes," they flash on the screen direct quotes from Darwin condemning "selfishness" as a "base principle" accounting for the "low morality of savages."

Skeptics, however—all with other worthwhile and needed planks of their own to push—immediately attacked this as questionable "cherry picking" out of the huge body of Darwin's original writings.

"If this is true," they charged, "with all the books written and courses taught about Darwin and evolution, why haven't we ever heard of this before? Does any scientist or educator of well-known and unquestionable status support this idea?"

In answer, progressive advocates flash on the screen pictures of the over fifty leading American, European, and Asian scientists and educators who comprise the Council of the Darwin Project advocating this shift for all levels of education.

Even so, with advocates for all the other planks competing for attention, the tide is turning against the progressives. Pointing out that the new Global Sounding measure of global health and wellbeing is based on the expanded new Darwinian perspective, they pass out copies for all to compare with their own better known alternatives during the luncheon break.

They also urge all to take a look on their lap tops at the website for The Darwin Project: www.thedarwinproject.com.

This was the advocates' composite analysis of the potential impact on education – and society – for the policies shift proposed.

MEASURING EVOLUTION

A GLOBAL SOUNDING OF THE IMPACT OF

[[Proposal to shift teaching of evolution in all schools in California from restriction to "first-half" Darwinism to full Darwinian theory of evolution]]

Levels of evolution	Indicators of progression (+)	Indicators of regression (-)	Enter impact (+, -, 0)
Cosmic	Sustainability of complex life forms	Environmental devastation	_____1_____
Chemical	Gaia hypothesis/ symbiosis	Environmental devastation	_____1_____
Biological	Health and longevity	Environmental devastation	_____1_____
BRAIN	**Parental love and nutrition**	**Lack of love and nutrition**	_____1_____
Psychological	Self-actualizing	Lack of fulfillment	_____1_____
[Cultural]	High priority for arts	Low priority for arts	_____1_____
Social	Freedom and equality	Control and inequality	_____1_____

Levels of evolution	Indicators of progression (+)	Indicators of regression (-)	Enter impact (+, -, 0)
Economic	Balanced private/public	Imbalanced private/public	_____0_____
Political	Democracy	Authoritarianism	_____1_____
Educational	Capacity for learning and independent thinking	Curtailing of facilities for learning and independent thinking	_____1_____
Technological	Emphasis on technologies of actualization	Emphasis on technologies of destruction	_____1_____
Moral	Living by the Golden Rule	Power of greed and corruption	_____1_____
Spiritual	Sense of identity with humanity and greater being	Slavery to materiality	_____1_____
Consciousness	Cognitive, affective, and conative scope	Curtailing of scope of mind	_____1_____
ACTION	Encouragement of progressive social action	Repression of progressive social action	_____1_____
	GLOBAL SOUNDING TOTAL		_____14_____

© David Loye 2006

MEASURING EVOLUTION

Strategies and Scenarios for Success

Comparison of Global Sounding results: For proposal to shift teaching of evolution in all schools in California from restriction to "first-half" Darwinism to full Darwinian theory of evolution, + 14.

Scenario: As everyone who, as a teacher, administrator, parent, or student at the high school or college level knows about the world of education, practically all decisions—other than mandates from legislatures or the bureaucratic top—are reached through the arguments and politics pro and con of advocates of various positions contending with one another.

In this example the Global Sounding is—and in most comparable examples will be—used by progressives in arguments to focus attention on factors that otherwise will be ignored or neglected in contention to win swing votes against the customary imbalance in power favoring defenders of the status quo.

In this example, when all participants returned to the discussion from the lunch break, during which they had a chance to examine the Global Sounding form expressing progressives' analysis, the opposition was first to speak.

"We agree that in the best of all possible worlds, with all the money in the world to spend, there should be more emphasis on the directions ostensibly supported by this interesting Global Sounding form. But this is not the best of all possible worlds, with darn little money left for education after all the billions going to an obscene investment in the military and the greed and corruption of the military-industrial complex. In one way or another we're already trying to move in these directions with what is already on the plate for education – and already badly needed. We fervently believe this proposal for one more new and untested venture should be shelved for now."

There now stepped forth for the progressives three members of the Darwin Project Council of over 50 leading American, European, and Asian scientists and educators advocating the shift – internationally known educators Nel Noddings of Columbia and the Stanford School of Education, Tim Seldin, president of the international Montessori Foundation, and Ron Miller, president of the Foundation for Educational Renewal. Each testified eloquently from their years of experience, but still the faces and the muttering indicated the outcome was in doubt.

End result: By a vote of 21 to 20, the progressives won and California became the first state to advocate – and then initiate – the shift from the "old" Darwin to the "new" Darwin throughout all levels of its schools.

MEDIA

Proposal: Newspaper, television, radio, and internet use of the Global Sounding as a regular feature for rating significance of news events.

Situation: Mettlenaught Media Group is the owner and manager of 14 newspapers, five radio stations, two television stations, and is venturing into internet nationally. A decision must be reached between investing in the Global Sounding or Grannie Hubbard's Tasty Tips as new features for all their holdings.

The Global Sounding offers a new way to expand the impact of what is ostensibly their primary function and service: to gather and report what's happening of potential significance in communities, nations, and the world. Grannie Hubbard's Tasty Tips offers nothing new, but is loaded with revenue-productive tie-in advertising possibilities.

The chief advocate for pilot testing the Global Sounding is Ransom Mettlenaught, 24-year-old grandson of media chain founder Myron Mettlenaught and newest member of the Board. Opposing him is C. McNeil Galsworthy, 70-year-old long time Board Chair, widely feared and respected figure in both national and global media circles.

"Are we to go on just being a lackluster copy-cat, regularly losing circulation to everybody else with any half-way fresh ideas?"

young Ransom asks the Board. "More importantly, at this time of mounting national and global crisis, when people everywhere are looking for some clue as to what the hell is going on, and how to get out of this mess, are we just to go on playing up scandals, and celebrity gossip, and catering to ignorance?"

CMG, as he is known throughout the industry, smiles indulgently.

"Fine words, Ransom. I'll grant you that. But as all we older heads around the table know, scandals, gossip, and ignorance are not only the butter for our own bread—they keep Mettlenaught Media Group up there in the Dow a good ways yet from bottom of the heap."

"But look at all we have to gain just in dollars and sense," Ransom argues. "The whole polling industry started out like this, and look at it today—both locally and globally one of the most closely followed and biggest generators of news; thereby building the circulation, which in turn pulls in and sets the mark for the advertising dollar. You mean to tell me, you don't believe regular Global Sounding ratings of the significance of events on the health and well-being of ourselves and our children can't be an immensely popular feature? Are our readers merely grazing cattle chewing the cud of whatever we feed them? Or do they have minds, and concerns about their children and the future? I sure care about mine!"

CMG's eyes narrow. His nose for potential power plays by would-be successors has kept him on top for forty years.

"If you want to play Woodward and Bernstein or Ed Murrow, go see a movie, Ransom," he says. "In the real world, as *we* know," he says, slowly scanning to look for eye contact with all around the table, "Grannie Hubbard's Tasty Tips may be a tame little copycat.

MEASURING EVOLUTION

But it can pull in the mountain of big advertising money from the biggies—Kraft, Kellogs, McDonalds, I suppose even *you* would know the rest."

CMG slams the table.

"That's the money that beats off the competition and keeps us here! And gentlemen, let me tell you, the goddam rumor's true. Rupert Murdoch is after our ass!"

Ransom merely rises and holds up his copies of the forms comparing Global Sounding with Grannie Hubbard.

"You've all got these copies. I urge you to think about your children, and your grandchildren, and carefully consider one versus the other. I move we briefly adjourn to do this."

The motion is seconded. And thirded. Confident of victory, but forced by the rules to submit, CMG declares a five minute recess.

A GLOBAL SOUNDING OF THE IMPACT OF

*[[Use of the Global Sounding as a Regular
Feature for Monitoring Significance of New Events]]*

Levels of evolution	Indicators of progression (+)	Indicators of regression (-)	Enter impact (+, -, 0)
Cosmic	Sustainability of complex life forms	Environmental devastation	_____1_____
Chemical	Gaia hypothesis/ symbiosis	Environmental devastation	_____1_____
Biological	Health and longevity	Environmental devastation	_____1_____
BRAIN	Parental love and nutrition	Lack of love and nutrition	_____1_____
Psychological	Self-actualizing	Lack of fulfillment	_____1_____
[Cultural]	High priority for arts	Low priority for arts	_____1_____
Social	Freedom and equality	Control and inequality	_____1_____

MEASURING EVOLUTION

Levels of evolution	Indicators of progression (+)	Indicators of regression (-)	Enter impact (+, -, 0)
Economic	Balanced private/public	Imbalanced private/public	_____1_____
Political	Democracy	Authoritarianism	_____1_____
Educational	Capacity for learning and independent thinking	Curtailing of facilities for learning and independent thinking	_____1_____
Technological	Emphasis on technologies of actualization	Emphasis on technologies of destruction	_____1_____
Moral	Living by the Golden Rule	Power of greed and corruption	_____1_____
Spiritual	Sense of identity with humanity and greater being	Slavery to materiality	_____1_____
Consciousness	Cognitive, affective, and conative scope	Curtailing of scope of mind	_____1_____
ACTION	Encouragement of progressive social action	Repression of progressive social action	_____1_____
	GLOBAL SOUNDING TOTAL		_____15_____

© David Loye 2006

DAVID LOYE

A GLOBAL SOUNDING OF THE IMPACT OF

[[*Grannie Hubbard's Tasty Tips as a Regular Feature for Mettlenaught Media Group Newspaper, Radio and Television Station, and New Internet Venture*]]

Levels of evolution	Indicators of progression (+)	Indicators of regression (-)	Enter impact (+, -, 0)
Cosmic	Sustainability of complex life forms	Environmental devastation	_____0_____
Chemical	Gaia hypothesis/ symbiosis	Environmental devastation	_____0_____
Biological	Health and longevity	Environmental devastation	_____0_____
BRAIN	Parental love and nutrition	Lack of love and nutrition	_____0_____
Psychological	Self-actualizing	Lack of fulfillment	_____0_____
[Cultural]	High priority for arts	Low priority for arts	_____0_____
Social	Freedom and equality	Control and inequality	_____0_____

MEASURING EVOLUTION

Levels of evolution	Indicators of progression (+)	Indicators of regression (-)	Enter impact (+, -, 0)
Economic	Balanced private/public	Imbalanced private/public	_____0_____
Political	Democracy	Authoritarianism	_____0_____
Educational	Capacity for learning and independent thinking	Curtailing of facilities for learning and independent thinking	_____0_____
Technological	Emphasis on technologies of actualization	Emphasis on technologies of destruction	_____0_____
Moral	Living by the Golden Rule	Power of greed and corruption	_____0_____
Spiritual	Sense of identity with humanity and greater being	Slavery to materiality	_____0_____
Consciousness	Cognitive, affective, and conative scope	Curtailing of scope of mind	_____0_____
ACTION	Encouragement of progressive social action	Repression of progressive social action	_____0_____
	GLOBAL SOUNDING TOTAL		_____0_____

© David Loye 2006

DAVID LOYE

Strategies and Scenarios for Success

Comparison of Global Sounding results: For Global Sounding, + 15. For Grannie Hubbard's Tasty Tips, 0.

Scenario: Within companies, in all except the most autocratic, decisions are reached through the arguments and politics pro and con of advocates of various positions against one another.

In this example the Global Sounding is—and in most comparable examples will be—used by progressives in arguments to focus attention on factors that otherwise will be ignored, neglected, or steam-rollered.

The goal is to win swing votes against the customary imbalance in power favoring defenders of the status quo and regressives.

In this example for Mettlenaught Media Group, on return from the five minute recess, CMG was astounded to find the board split evenly pro and con Global Sounding. Realizing he needed to do some hasty private arm-twisting and fence-mending, he immediately suggested the Board adjourn to privately further consider the matter, then return in two weeks to reach a decision.

But now something wholly unexpected happened to confound CMG anew. For Ransom's public relations agent got the word out and suddenly in *Publisher's Weekly* and the *Wall Street Journal* long articles appeared playing up the juicy news of the Old Boy-Young Turk struggle at Mettlenaught and the impending Murdoch take-over try.

Most disturbing was the advocacy by Bill Moyers, Walter

MEASURING EVOLUTION

Cronkite, Ted Turner, and George Soros for a bold pilot testing of the Global Sounding in hard-hitting articles that got an enormous play on the internet.

End results: The Mettlenaught Media Group Board surprised everybody—including both young Ransom and CMG—by voting to okay Grannie for publications and stations in ho-hum areas for their circulation, but okayed the Global Sounding for a chain-wise pilot test in their more lively, interesting, and progressive areas.

"It's a hopeful foot in the door," was Moyers' comment. "Good news for democracy," trumpeted Turner, Soros, and Al Gore.

A NON-PROFIT ORGANIZATION

Proposal: Expand funding for a project and program aimed at the reduction of intimate violence—that is, violence in the home against women and children.

Situation: Some very difficult decisions must be reached among a bewildering variety of obviously worthwhile proposals by the staff, director, and board for the annual allocation of $2,000,000 by the Gwendoln Martin MacReady Foundation.

In the case of the intimate violence reduction proposal, advocates point to the devastating impact of violence in the home on the mental, emotional, and behavioral development of children. They further show the powerful link that research reveals of violence in the home to the devastating impact on our world of war and all other forms of grown-up violence in communities and nations. Advocates urge all involved in the decision to view the case made by the eloquent writings of cultural evolution theorist Riane Eisler and the website for the Spiritual Alliance to End Intimate Violence (SAIV): www.saiv.org.

"It's certainly an appealing proposal," foundation director Maude Markham remarks to her fellow decision-makers after this presentation, "but what about all the rest? This pilot proposal to fund school lunches in Alabama? More money for science teachers? This very appealing proposal for scholarships for outstanding teachers to gain M.A.'s and Ph.D.'s? And so many, many more. I'm frankly at sea on how best to proceed this year."

At this point, advocates for the intimate violence reduction project proposed an experimental use by the Foundation of the new Global Sounding measure of global health and well-being. They explained how it was designed to help Foundations decide among the usual overwhelming number of worthy projects, how to use it, and passed out forms enough to cover all projects under consideration.

"This looks like a good idea," Maude Markham said. "We'll adjourn to see how much good in the world we think each of these projects can do, and then come back to compare results."

This was the composite result for the intimate violence reduction project.

DAVID LOYE

A GLOBAL SOUNDING OF THE IMPACT OF

[[Funding a project to reduce violence against women and children in the home – and thereby the larger world]]

Levels of evolution	Indicators of progression (+)	Indicators of regression (-)	Enter impact (+, -, 0)
Cosmic	Sustainability of complex life forms	Environmental devastation	0
Chemical	Gaia hypothesis/ symbiosis	Environmental devastation	0
Biological	Health and longevity	Environmental devastation	1
BRAIN	Parental love and nutrition	Lack of love and nutrition	1
Psychological	Self-actualizing	Lack of fulfillment	1
[Cultural]	High priority for arts	Low priority for arts	0
Social	Freedom and equality	Control and inequality	1

MEASURING EVOLUTION

Levels of evolution	Indicators of progression (+)	Indicators of regression (-)	Enter impact (+, -, 0)
Economic	Balanced private/public	Imbalanced private/public	_____0_____
Political	Democracy	Authoritarianism	_____1_____
Educational	Capacity for learning and independent thinking	Curtailing of facilities for learning and independent thinking	_____1_____
Technological	Emphasis on technologies of actualization	Emphasis on technologies of destruction	_____1_____
Moral	Living by the Golden Rule	Power of greed and corruption	_____1_____
Spiritual	Sense of identity with humanity and greater being	Slavery to materiality	_____1_____
Consciousness	Cognitive, affective, and conative scope	Curtailing of scope of mind	_____1_____
ACTION	Encouragement of progressive social action	Repression of progressive social action	_____1_____
	GLOBAL SOUNDING TOTAL		_____11_____

© David Loye 2006

DAVID LOYE

Among Other Contending Proposals

To save space and provide ease of comparison, we're giving the scores by themselves rather than in the form.

✱

Form for: [Pilot proposal to fund school lunches in Alabama].

Cosmic: 0. Chemical: 0. Biological: 1. Brain: 1. Psychological: 1. Cultural: 0. Social: 1. Economic: 0. Political: 0. Educational: 1. Technological: 1. Moral: 1. Spiritual: 0. Consciousness: 1. Action: 0.

Global Sounding Total: **+ 8**

✱

Form for: [More money for science teachers].

Cosmic: 1. Chemical: 1. Biological: 1. Brain: 0. Psychological: 0. Cultural: 0. Social: 0. Economic: 0. Political: 0. Educational: 1. Technological: 1. Moral: 1. Spiritual: 0. Consciousness: 1. Action: 0.

Global Sounding Total: **+ 7**

✱

Form for: [Scholarships for outstanding teachers to gain M.A.s and Ph.D.s].

MEASURING EVOLUTION

Cosmic: 1. Chemical: 1. Biological: 1. Brain: 1. Psychological: 1. Cultural: 1. Social: 1. Economic: 0. Political: 1. Educational: 1. Technological: 1. Moral: 0. Spiritual: 0. Consciousness: 1. Action: 0.

Global Sounding Total: + 11

✻

Strategies and Scenarios for Success

Comparison of Global Sounding results: For proposal to expand funding for a project and program aimed at the reduction of intimate violence, + *11.* For pilot proposal to fund school lunches in Alabama, + *8.* For more money for science teachers, + *7.* For scholarships for outstanding teachers to gain M.A. s and Ph.D. s, + *11.*

Scenario: As everyone who, as director, staff, or board members knows about the world of foundations and other non profit organizations, practically all decisions are reached through the opinions pro and con of advocates of various positions respectfully contending with one another.

In this example the Global Sounding is—and in most comparable examples will be—used by progressives to focus attention on factors that otherwise could be ignored or neglected within the give and take generally favoring defenders of the "safe," "tried and true," or status quo positions.

In this case, all involved were fascinated by the fact that the composite results helped definitely rule out two of the proposals, but left the intimate violence reduction proposal tied with scholarships for outstanding teachers to gain M.A.'s and Ph.D.'s, each with a score of + 11.

End result*:* Out of the ensuing discussion came two fascinating results. First, they decided to fund both the violence reduction and the scholarships for teachers proposals. Second, all were so delighted with the utility of the new Global Sounding measure they voted to make it a standard evaluation instrument for all subsequent staff and board meetings.

Director Maude Markham was indeed so enthusiastic she wrote an article about successful use of the new measure for non-profit decision-making processes for *Philanthropy* magazine. She also gave a very popular talk about and workshop on use of the Global Sounding at the Annual Conference of the Council on Foundations.

As this became a typical result for the enthusiasm of an expanding number of non-profits, use of the Global Sounding spread so rapidly internationally that the Spencer Foundation funded research to track and unequivocally measure impact of use of the new measure on actual human evolutionary advance.

A RELIGIOUS ORGANIZATION

Proposal: Shift from attack on the "old" amoral Darwinian model for evolution to qualified support for the expanded new Darwinian model advancing moral as well as spiritual evolution.

Situation: The conflict between Creationists fervently seeking to burn and advocates of Intelligent Design ostensibly seeking to build a bridge to science from religion has reached a new decision point in the United Churches of Jesus Christ the Only Savior, with a national congregation reportedly of one million.

A sincerely scientifically oriented but only barely tolerated faction with the Intelligent Designists advocates use of the new Global Sounding measure to reveal the potential common ground between science and religion to all involved.

"We see this as being a moral-action-oriented instrument developed by scientists reaching out to try to end the old conflict between science and religion. We must respond, in turn, by reaching back in recognition there may be a common cause beyond disagreements here."

Those against the proposal, however, refuse to have anything to do with this heresy or its Satanic Global Sounding form. Advocates for the proposal then argue that the fact of recognition among scientists of the urgent need and a clear commonality of goals for moral and spiritual evolution should be welcomed rather than attacked.

They are joined in making their case by three leading scientists who make clear that *while they wholly disagree with both Creationism and Intelligent Design as functionally anti-scientific movements,* the challenge faced by our species during the 21st century is so great that, if the threat of ultimate annihilation is to be met, science and religion must somehow find ways of working together, rather than against each other.

Advocates urge all present to set aside prior fixed beliefs and consider their following evaluation of the Darwinian "shift" proposal.

MEASURING EVOLUTION

A GLOBAL SOUNDING OF THE IMPACT OF

[[Shift from attack on the "old" Darwinian model for evolution to qualified support for the expanded new Darwinian model supporting moral as well as spiritual goals]]

Levels of evolution	Indicators of progression (+)	Indicators of regression (-)	Enter impact (+, -, 0)
Cosmic	Sustainability of complex life forms	Environmental devastation	_____1_____
Chemical	Gaia hypothesis/ symbiosis	Environmental devastation	_____1_____
Biological	Health and longevity	Environmental devastation	_____1_____
BRAIN	**Parental love and nutrition**	**Lack of love and nutrition**	_____1_____
Psychological	Self-actualizing	Lack of fulfillment	_____1_____
[Cultural]	High priority for arts	Low priority for arts	_____1_____
Social	Freedom and equality	Control and inequality	_____1_____

DAVID LOYE

Levels of evolution	Indicators of progression (+)	Indicators of regression (-)	Enter impact (+, -, 0)
Economic	Balanced private/public	Imbalanced private/public	____1____
Political	Democracy	Authoritarianism	____1____
Educational	Capacity for learning and independent thinking	Curtailing of facilities for learning and independent thinking	____1____
Technological	Emphasis on technologies of actualization	Emphasis on technologies of destruction	____1____
Moral	Living by the Golden Rule	Power of greed and corruption	____1____
Spiritual	Sense of identity with humanity and greater being	Slavery to materiality	____1____
Consciousness	Cognitive, affective, and conative scope	Curtailing of scope of mind	____1____
ACTION	Encouragement of progressive social action	Repression of progressive social action	____1____
	GLOBAL SOUNDING TOTAL		____15____

© David Loye 2006

MEASURING EVOLUTION

Strategies and Scenarios for Success

Consideration of Global Sounding results: For the proposal to shift from attack against the old Darwinian model to qualified support for the new Darwinian model, + *15.*

Scenario: As everyone who, as a minister, bishop, archbishop, rabbi, imam, priest, guru, monk or nun knows about the world of religions, practically all decisions—other than in fiat from above in certain faiths—are reached through the opinions pro and con of advocates of various positions contending with one another.

In this example the Global Sounding is—and in most comparable examples will be—used by progressives to focus attention on factors that otherwise could be ignored or neglected within the give and take generally favoring defenders of the "safe," "tried and true" status quo, or unfortunately, fierce and virulently regressive positions.

In this case, it had been expected the proposal would either be quickly laughed or shouted out of consideration. A surprise emerged, however. A significant number of evangelical Creationists, as well as Intelligent Designists, as well as some general congregation members rose up and insisted the proposal be given serious consideration because of the recognition by their church leaders of the rapidly mounting threat of global warming to all humanity and the planet.

"We have examined this instrument," they said, "and we find it is not only unusually sensitive to the global environment threat but also to the need for moral and spiritual evolution. This is serious, friends. Much as the idea might choke in our throats, the threat to human survival that science is documenting is real, and we've got to somehow find a way to work together or we face Armageddon for sure."

There were those who stood up to cry out, "Why delay the Rapture any longer? Let's dump the sinful mess of this world and gain the Heavenly Kingdom!" "Hear! Hear!" "Bring it on!" But by and large the meeting became more subdued and thoughtful.

End result: By a vote of 60 to 20, the proposal was voted down. But under the circumstances the advocates rejoiced. "The ice has been broken," one remarked. "They're beginning to think."

With the mounting exposure of the deceit and corruption and just plain incompetence of both the political and religious leaders they had been following, it was felt the majority could be ready to swing the other way next time.

All agreed that the tactic to take was to encourage as much experimental use as possible of the Global Sounding by reasonably progressive ministers in cases of less loaded group decision-making, come back next year with the same proposal with a video of prestigious evangelical supporters to display to the assembly, and try again.

A PHILANTHROPIST WITH A FOUNDATION

Proposal: Invest in a project to positively re-align and accelerate human evolution with a full spectrum, action-oriented, and reconstructed Darwinian theory of evolution.

Situation: On the death of her husband, Roland, Meg Randall has been left with a fortune, a foundation the two of them founded, and a dream of investing in a scientific project hard for most to understand, but calculated to radically change the world for the better. With many decades behind it of advanced social and systems scientific research in evolution by thousands of scientists internationally, it is a complex project proposed by evolutionary systems scientist David Loye.

In essence, it outlines a way to help effect a shift from the socially, economically, and politically disastrous old Darwinian paradigm of "survival of the fittest" and "selfishness above all" to the social, economic, and political liberation of a reconstructed new "full spectrum" and action-oriented Darwinian theory and story of human evolution.

To explain her proposal to the board of directors for the Crysalis Foundation that she and her late husband had founded, Meg uses the Global Sounding form. She shows how the fifteen indicators of positive or negative impact on human evolution reflect the new "full spectrum," action-oriented Darwinian theory.

She tells of how finding out about the Global Sounding measure, and becoming intrigued with it, led her first to the website of The Darwin Project (www.thedarwinproject.com) and then to "a remarkable book by a number of scientists called *The Great Adventure: Toward a Fully Human Theory of Evolution*, which lays out the plan I want to fund."

"The beauty of it," she explains, "is that this new work, with thousands of progressive studies behind it, provides us with a new scientifically grounded guide for getting out of the mess we're in and at last more effectively building the better future. It's like the difference between having a road map to where we want to go versus floundering around in a highway system full of potholes and endless detours without road signs or signals."

The board chair, Bork Brankenshift, rises to glance about the board in a way suggesting he speaks for all, then leans toward her with a patronizing smile.

"We're sure you mean well, Meg," she is astounded to hear him say, "but we just can't go on being asked to buy another pig in the poke."

Furious at the unexpected gall and disrespect of the man, Meg distributes her own Global Sounding assessment of the project, which follows, and stalks from the room. Looking over the form, the faces of the board members variously reflect interest, skepticism, bewilderment, and discomfort.

MEASURING EVOLUTION

A GLOBAL SOUNDING OF THE IMPACT OF

[[Funding the development of a full-spectrum, action-oriented and reconstructed Darwinian theory of human evolution]]

Levels of evolution	Indicators of progression (+)	Indicators of regression (-)	Enter impact (+, -, 0)
Cosmic	Sustainability of complex life forms	Environmental devastation	_____1_____
Chemical	Gaia hypothesis/ symbiosis	Environmental devastation	_____1_____
Biological	Health and longevity	Environmental devastation	_____1_____
BRAIN	**Parental love and nutrition**	**Lack of love and nutrition**	_____1_____
Psychological	Self-actualizing	Lack of fulfillment	_____1_____
[Cultural]	High priority for arts	Low priority for arts	_____1_____
Social	Freedom and equality	Control and inequality	_____1_____

DAVID LOYE

Levels of evolution	Indicators of progression (+)	Indicators of regression (-)	Enter impact (+, -, 0)
Economic	Balanced private/public	Imbalanced private/public	_____1_____
Political	Democracy	Authoritarianism	_____1_____
Educational	Capacity for learning and independent thinking	Curtailing of facilities for learning and independent thinking	_____1_____
Technological	Emphasis on technologies of actualization	Emphasis on technologies of destruction	_____1_____
Moral	Living by the Golden Rule	Power of greed and corruption	_____1_____
Spiritual	Sense of identity with humanity and greater being	Slavery to materiality	_____1_____
Consciousness	Cognitive, affective, and conative scope	Curtailing of scope of mind	_____1_____
ACTION	Encouragement of progressive social action	Repression of progressive social action	_____1_____
	GLOBAL SOUNDING TOTAL		_____15_____

© David Loye 2006

MEASURING EVOLUTION

Strategies and Scenarios for Success

Global Sounding result: For the proposal to fund the development of a full-spectrum, action-oriented and reconstructed Darwinian theory of human evolution, + *15.*

Scenario: In this example, something was happening behind the scenes that occurs in clashes between regressive boards and ambitious directors and progressive founders far more frequently than most people realize. Acting as classic examples themselves of the old Darwinian paradigm of "survival of the fittest" and "selfishness above all," an ultra-conservative faction within the board had decided to seize power from Roland Randall's "feminist" and "pinko" widow Meg. (For the real life case on which this example is based, see *Bankrolling Evolution,* chapter six, for the heroic story of Irene Diamond and her fight to regain control of her own money from a board coup d'etat. See, also, chapter nine in *The Great Adventure: Toward a Fully Human Theory of Evolution*, as well as The Darwin Project website (www.thedarwinproject.com) for detailed explanations of Meg's proposal).

Led by Bork Brankenshift, in a narrow vote the board not only voted down Meg's proposal but effectively seized control of her own foundation from her. Rather than back down, Meg launched a battle against them in court and joined in employing independent accountants to investigate the board predators, in particular Bork Brankenshift.

End result: Just as happened with Irene Diamond, Meg not only legally won back control of her foundation, and not only went on to form another more progressive foundation. She and all her supporters had the satisfaction of seeing Bork Brankenshift arrested and imprisoned for embezzlement (yes, this actually happened in real life).

Throughout the battle, Meg and her supporters frequently turned to use of the Global Sounding measure to get across the importance of the project she had been proposing. With full control of her new foundation, with progressives for all board members, the Global Sounding theory-building project was finally launched. And with continuing funding from Meg and many other progressive philanthropists and foundations, it became a significant force in the upgrading, renewal, and prosocial impact of the American and global mind.

CODA: AN OVERVIEW

These, of course, are fictional examples. But they are constructed to provide insights and guidance for effective use of the Global Sounding measure in a wide variety of situations faced by progressives in business, government, politics, science, education, the media, nonprofit and religious organizations, and philanthropists.

As can be seen from these examples, opponents of the use of the Global Sounding form could accuse proponents of results being biased, subjective, and open to manipulation.

The fact is this is actually more or less true not only of science, but of everything else one gathers to present to make a case for what one believes to be needed and rightful.

As we have seen, what is ostensibly supposed to exist as a great pure and sacred body of pristine fact in real life sorts out into the progressive science that drives human evolution ahead, the status quo science that checks it in place, or the regressive science that drives us backward.

For more on the case for the scientist as activist—*and thereby an urgently needed partisan*—see Chapter Six, Global Healing: the Challenge to Money, Science, Sense, and Sanity.

Among other justifications and uses for the Global Sounding measure, advocates can also point out that the Global Sounding scale can provide a highly useful guide for structuring economic and productive discussions aimed at reaching the best decisions.

Some old hands particularly experienced in the decision process -- with jaundiced views of what has wasted time in the past – could also point this out.

Using the Global Sounding Scale can certainly be a big improvement over the customary practice of hiring a coterie of consultants to take months in evaluations.

Which can result in the investment of a great deal of time by high wage business, governmental, foundation, or other personnel and board members.

With a total expense item for consultants and organizational time of potentially many thousands of dollars.

All of which might otherwise have gone to worthy and generally very needy projects.

With all too generally what proves to be a long dull report that few read at the end of the line. Which almost no one can really understand. And which in the end, with bad feelings about the whole thing, is junked and everybody just goes on playing it by ear or winging the decisions as usual.

In the end, it can be a question of where one's loyalties lie: to the better future, to things as they are, or to the worst of our past.

SIX   GLOBAL HEALING: THE CHALLENGE TO MONEY, SCIENCE, SENSE, AND SANITY

"Not only will wildlife and whole ecosystems go extinct, but in human civilization the planet has a precious resource.

"We are not merely a disease; we are, through our intelligence and communication, the nervous system of the planet. Through us, Gaia has seen herself from space, and begins to know her place in the universe.

"We should be the heart and mind of the Earth, not its malady. So let us be brave . . . and see that we have harmed the living Earth and need to make our peace with Gaia. We must do it while we are still strong enough to negotiate, and not a broken rabble led by brutal war lords.

"Most of all, we should remember that we are a part of it, and it is indeed our home."

These are the closing lines for British scientist and Gaia theorist James Lovelock's passionate plea for global healing in 2006.

One may disagree with some of his views on specifics, but the potential horror of his vision and the urgent case for action is unquestionable.

As spelled out in our End Document reprint of his full statement, in effect Lovelock warns that unless we much more rapidly shift from "business as usual" to multinational global healing our planet will soon face the ecological equivalent of "a morbid fever that may last as long as 100,000 years."

Lovelock is a prime case in point of how at this crucial juncture in evolution we waver between reclamation and disaster. The "Gaia hypothesis" of our planet as a living system, which must be treated and respected as such, was first advanced by Lovelock during the 1960s, then in the 1970s biologist Lynn Margulis joined as his chief collaborator in advancing it. Since then "Gaia theory" has often been mocked and resisted by the status quo in science and society. But in another rapidly growing part of science, and among the so-called general population, the feeling escalates that the Gaia theory is very much on target.[14]

In addition to being based on the long ignored rest of Darwin and advanced work in all the other fields of science outlined in our text and End Documents, The Global Sounding is very much attuned to the Gaia theory. As such, it is in a position similar to that of Lovelock and Margulis starting out.

In other words, as indicated earlier, the Global Sounding is sure to come under fire from regressives. More serious to consider at this stage, however, are the legitimate questions and criticisms of responsible methodologists. In Further Developmental Considerations in our End Documents we answer questions they're likely to raise.

MEASURING EVOLUTION

The Battle Within and Around Science for the Future for Our Species and Our Planet

The main aspect of the Global Sounding likely to draw the fire of the defenders of the science of the status quo, however, will be the charge that the Global Sounding is an inexcusable lapse from the impartiality and objectivity that are supposed to govern the true scientist in all ventures.

This charge not only against the Global Sounding but for anything else like it must be answered, and squarely and firmly. Otherwise, progressive organizations whose purposes could be greatly advanced by use of the Global Sounding, to the benefit of all of us, will be diverted by bad advice.

The main problem here is "politics."

That is, what the defenders of the science of the status quo may focus on in this case is that the development of The Global Sounding as a measure came out of the research that also led to the writing of *Measuring Evolution's* inevitably controversial companion *Bankrolling Evolution: Money, Science, and Politics.*

In the best of all possible worlds the Global Sounding would have emerged as pure and virginal as supposedly the goddess Athena from the brow of Zeus. But unfortunately ours is not only far from being such a world. As the matrix for the Bush policies pilot study shows in chapter three, we're dangerously moving away from rather than toward that best of all possible worlds.

The problem for many defenders of the status quo is that science is supposed to be "above the taint of politics."

In other words, within the structure for science still prevailing as we enter the 21st century all its fields still tend to be protectively walled off from one another in separate baronies, or educational boxes, with the idea that the troublesome topic of politics must be comfortably relegated solely to the box called "political science."

This may seem to be a small matter, but its consequences for society are enormous.

Over the years men like biologist Julian Huxley and anthropologist Ashley Montagu, women like biologist Rachel Carson and anthropologist Margaret Meade, and organizations like the Union of Concerned Scientists and the Bulletin of Atomic Scientists have fought to provide science with a voice that could help shape progressive social, economic, and political policies. But even theirs have generally been lonely and scattered voices, either widely ignored or fiercely resisted by the science of the status quo and "the powers that be."

For lesser known scientists in all fields the message has been clear. Most scientists are generally on the payroll of an institution that has to be careful, or are funded by foundations leery of controversy, so one learns to bellyache in private but never speak out.

In contrast to earlier times, by now even the political scientist will hesitate before writing directly and bluntly of what one actually perceives and believes these days.

Yet here our species is entering the greatest crisis in human evolution and the voices of the experts best qualified to provide guidance—as practically on a daily basis Bush administration policies dramatized—are routinely being stilled.

Yet if ever a time has arrived for scientists to abide by the higher rule of conscience and speak frankly and openly of what their expertise in measurement or any other aspect of science reveals, this

MEASURING EVOLUTION

is it.

As Regression Machine policies threaten to divert America from its historical role in human evolution, it has become a matter of urgency for nonscientists as well as scientists to understand the crucial difference, as outlined in *Bankrolling Evolution*, between progressive, status quo, and regressive science and education.

What is and what isn't science is everywhere blurred today by the regressive art of using what one claims to be science to obfuscate, intimidate, divert, or shut off discussion of any threat to the status quo.

The targeted heretic is bombarded with accusations of not being "empirical," lacking "control groups," but most effectively of not being sufficiently "objective." To some the worst of all scientific sins is to be, God forbid, "subjective."

For this reason it is vital for both nonscientists and scientists who have not really thought much about this to realize that the ideal of "pure objectivity," which supposedly is to imprison us forever, arose out of the so-called hard sciences, where one is dealing with atoms or controlled experiments with microbes and such.

But in the radically different territory of the so-called soft sciences—which deal with human activities; that is, the social sciences, the systems sciences, and the new field of evolutionary systems science, which deal with *human* evolution—*subjectivity* as well as objectivity is a basic requirement.

Many great social scientists—e.g., Gunnar Myrdal, Abraham Maslow—have made the point I am making here.[15] As anthropologist Hortense Powdermaker expressed it, one works to uncover the "truth" as both stranger and friend.[16] One becomes the objective onlooker, the *stranger*. But one also becomes the insider capable of feeling the pain, the joy, the rage, or any other motivating thought and feeling moving within those one is trying to work with or understand, as their *friend*.

Today, however, we live in a time of such escalating threats to our species and to our planet that, beyond what was normal for science earlier, the role of both stranger and friend has radically changed.

Increasingly, the scientist and the educator—and every one of us who cares about these matters—faces the need for sensitivity to the historical and evolutionary situation of our species and the requirement of a much larger role.

The new role is of both stranger and friend as *partisan*—that is, of a scientific and educational commitment to openly and devoutly put one's expertise and voice to the cause of human advancement.

It is the commitment to serve, if necessary, as a guerilla fighter for humanity.

Beyond matters of methodology, which can be improved as we go, and beyond matters of politics, which it is designed to embrace and transcend, this is the intended driving role and loyalty for the Global Sounding.

Some Bedrock Conclusions

***First*:** The evolution of our species and of all life on this planet, if not indeed the planet itself, is clearly at stake in choices still everywhere being made *for* us, rather than *by* us.

Second: All things considered, as *Bankrolling Evolution* and by now books, speeches, and manifestos of hundreds of scientists underlines,[17] the thrust driving the over 100,000 year evolution of our particular species, homo sapiens sapiens, has done a reasonably good job

MEASURING EVOLUTION

of pushing us uphill toward the better world. *But our time is running out.*

The results of the pilot test for the Global Sounding reflect not just our current situation. *They signal the recurring pattern that lies ahead for the 21st century unless the regressive detour from the open highway laid out by evolution is shut off and our journey into the future is set back on track.*

As was the conclusion for *Bankrolling Evolution*, these first results for the Global Sounding underline the evolutionary call for a Progressive Alliance of progressive money, progressive science, progressive politics, progressive economics, progressive education, progressive morality, progressive spirituality, and progressive entertainment to recapture and advance the vision of Pericles' Athens. And of Minoan Crete, Mohenjendaro, and Harrapa. And of Jesus, Gautama, and Hildegarde of Bingen. And of the Islam of the age of Ibn Khaldun, the Renaissance, the 18th century Enlightenment, and of the original American revolution on the behalf of all humanity.

It's time to wake and work on behalf of the ancient dream of the better world that is now *our* responsibility to nurture, protect, and to advance.

Or in disgrace beyond expression, stand by while bit by bit it is ended.

End Documents

THE GLOBAL SOUNDING MORAL CODE

The Global Sounding is a new measure of global health and well-being based on the findings of great progressive scientists and their successors over at least two hundred years.

Out of this span of time for scientific studies and the comparatively recent development of evolutionary systems science outlined in *Measuring Evolution* and *Bankrolling Evolution*, a recent multidisciplinary study (*The Great Adventure: Toward a Fully Human Theory of Evolution* [SUNY Press, 2004]) identified fifteen levels and activities for evolution.

For each of the fifteen levels and activities, the Global Sounding identifies *indicators of progression*—measuring *advance* for human evolution; *indicators of regression*—measuring movement backward; and the resulting degree to which we are moving forward, are being checked in place, or are being shoved backward in evolution.

※

In keeping with the emphasis of progressive religion over thousands of years, of progressive science over hundreds of years, and especially, with shocking impact and implications, of Charles Darwin's long ignored emphasis on *moral evolution* as the core drive for *human evolution*, development of the Global Sounding provides a well-grounded basis for a scientific statement of what is right and what is wrong for the development and destiny of our species.

In other words, this new measure has been developed in response to the need for an updated, cross-culturally relevant, potentially widely acceptable "global ethic" articulated by the Union of Concerned Scientists, speaking for the global scientific community, and the World Parliament of Religions, speaking for the global religious community.

In effect a statement of the "secular morality" also called for by the Dalai Lama, the Global Sounding Moral Code has been developed not to replace but to augment earlier statements of progressive religions with an experimental scientific statement of what is moral, or right or wrong.

※

We'll first state the Code.

Then we'll show how the fifteen statements for the Global Sounding Moral Code were derived from the fifteen levels and activities for evolution, along with indicators for progression and indicators for regression.

Certain items will likely seem rather mystifying at first. For explanations, see chapters one through three and End Document "The Scientific and Political Grounding for the Sounding" for *Measuring Evolution.*

Then to provide the vital context of the American and global political realities needed to give these moral concepts the driving edge for moral action, we'll indicate their derivation also from the results of the Global Sounding pilot study of G.W.Bush presidential and Republican congressional majority policies.

See chapter three in this book for the Bush policies pilot study report. See ending chapters of *Bankrolling Evolution* for some implications for political, economic, and moral action.

MEASURING EVOLUTION

I. The Code

1

Honor and respect rather than plunder and rape our living environment.

2

Honor and respect Earth as the Mother of us all rather than sell her into slavery.

3

100 years of science tells us Earth can still provide the resources for health for all of us if given a fair and practical human distribution system. Establishing health systems for the many rather than the chosen few is the moral requirement, and must be our goal.

4

100 years of science tells us that a healthy brain and
healthy mind depends on adequate food
and love in childhood.
Thus nurturing and expanding, rather than
starving and blighting, is the moral requirement
for the feeding of brain and mind,
which must be our goal.

5

Mind is the precious gift of life to be nurtured, enlightened,
and celebrated, rather than orphaned at birth and
thereafter degraded and exploited.

6

Culture is *the most precious gift of evolution,*
to be cherished and nurtured in the wonder of its diversity,
rather than seized, shucked and twisted to serve low ends.

MEASURING EVOLUTION

7

Over thousands of years freedom and equality have been
and will remain the most precious goals for evolution,
rather than just words to be used by power-mad
deceivers to sell control and inequality.

8

Three hundred years of capitalism and two hundred years
of communism have shown us that a fair, peaceful, and
practical distribution of Earth's bounty requires
a balance of public and private governance,
rather than the breeding of misery, war, and
corruption with a shift in overwhelming
power to one or the other.

9

Democracy,
rather than the sham of the oligarchy of
wealth, the creep by stealth toward
fascism, or the prison of
any other form of tyranny, is a moral requirement,
and must be our goal.

10

Education for all,
rather than the fact of good schools for some
and bad schools or no schools for all
others, is a moral requirement,
which must be our goal.

11

Develop technologies to strengthen and expand the voices
of caring and reason and the abundance of life,
rather than technologies that ever more
powerfully threaten to, and indeed then
are driven to, launch and kill life

12

Differently stated but the same for all, the message
of thousands of studies of progressive science is exactly
the same as for thousands of years for progressive religion:
Do unto others as ye would have them do unto you—rather than
do it unto others before they can do it unto you.

MEASURING EVOLUTION

13

Affirm our identity but also our responsibility in tandem
with a greater being, a greater reality, or a greater
mission, rather than fool yourself by claiming
some one and only holy being, idea, or cause
for your own low ends.

14

The most precious gift of evolution is consciousness.
Love, nurture, and expand it, rather than
automatically seek to narrow, blunt,
or otherwise slap it into shape
and seize the pitiful remnant
for your own low ends.

15

For over 100,000 years the choice before our species
has been unchanging. Either join those who take action
on behalf of the better world, or fall back in shame or ignorance
with those willing to sell out to the highest bidder and
join the march to extinction.

DAVID LOYE

II. Derivation of the Code from Evolutionary Indicators for the Global Sounding Measure of Global Well-Being

Cosmic Evolution. For the Global Sounding measure of global well-being, see "Global Sounding Matrix and User Form" in these End Documents for handy reference. As shown there within the full context for the measure, "Sustainability of complex life forms" is the chosen indicator of *progression*. "Environmental devastation" is the indicator of *regression*. Thus, for the Moral Code the indicator of *progression* for the Measure becomes this statement for the Code:

Code 1: *For Cosmic Evolution*: Honor and respect rather than plunder and rape our living environment.

✹

Chemical Evolution. "Gaia hypothesis, symbiosis" is the indicator of progression. "Environmental devastation" is the indicator of regression. Thus the indicator of progression for the Measure becomes this statement for the Code:

Code 2: *For Chemical Evolution*: Honor and respect Earth as the Mother of us all rather than sell her into slavery.

✹

MEASURING EVOLUTION

Biological Evolution. "Health and longevity" is the indicator of progression. "Environmental devastation" is the indicator of regression. The indicator of progression for the Measure becomes this statement for the Code:

Code 3: *For Biological Evolution*: 100 years of science tells us Earth can still provide the resources for health for all of us if given a fair and practical human distribution system. Establishing health systems for the many rather than the chosen few is the moral requirement, and must be our goal.

✺

Evolution of the Brain. "Parental love and nutrition" is the indicator of progression. "Lack of love and nutrition" is the indicator of regression. The indicator of progression for the Measure becomes this statement for the Code:

Code 4: *For Evolution of the Brain*: 100 years of science tells us that a healthy brain and healthy mind depends on adequate food and love in childhood. Thus nurturing and expanding, rather than starving and blighting, is the moral requirement for the feeding of brain and mind, which must be our goal.

✺

Psychological Evolution. "Self-actualizing" is the indicator of progression. "Lack of fulfillment" is the indicator of regression. The indicator of progression becomes this statement for the Code:

Code 5: *For Psychological Evolution*: Mind is the precious gift of life to be nurtured, enlightened, and celebrated, rather than orphaned at birth and thereafter degraded and exploited.

✺

Cultural Evolution. "High priority for arts" is the indicator of progression. "Low priority for arts" is the indicator of regression. The indicator of progression for the Measure becomes this statement for the Code:

Code 6: *For Cultural Evolution*: Culture is *the most precious gift of evolution* to be cherished and nurtured in the wonder of its diversity, rather than seized, shucked and twisted to serve low ends.

✺

Social Evolution. "Freedom and equality" is the indicator for progression. "Control and inequality" is the indicator for regression. The indicator of progression for the Measure becomes this statement for the Code:

Code 7: *For Social Evolution:* Over thousands of years freedom and equality have been and will remain the most precious goals for evolution, rather than just words to be used by power-mad deceivers to sell control and inequality.

✺

MEASURING EVOLUTION

Economic Evolution. "Balanced private/public" is the indicator for progression. "Imbalanced private/public" is the indicator for regression. The indicator of progression becomes this statement for the Code:

Code 8: *For Economic Evolution*: Three hundred years of capitalism and two hundred years of communism have shown us that a fair, peaceful, and practical distribution of Earth's bounty requires a balance of public and private governance, rather than the breeding of misery, war, and corruption with a shift in overwhelming power to one or the other.

※

Political Evolution. "Democracy" is the indicator of progression. "Authoritarianism" is the indicator of regression. The indicator of progression for the Measure becomes this statement for the Code:

Code 9: *For Political Evolution*: Democracy, rather than the sham of the oligarchy of wealth, the creep by stealth toward fascism, or the prison of any other form of tyranny, is a moral requirement, and must be our goal.

※

Educational Evolution. "Capacity for learning and independent thinking" is the indicator for progression. "Curtailing of facilities for learning and independent thinking" is the indicator of regression. The indicator of progression for the Measure becomes this statement for the Code:

Code 10: *For Educational Evolution*: Education for all, rather than the fact of good schools for some and bad schools or no schools for all others, is a moral requirement, which must be our goal.

✷

Technological Evolution. "Emphasis on technologies of actualization" is the indicator of progression. "Emphasis on technologies of destruction" is the indicator of regression. The indicator of progression for the Measure becomes this statement for the Code:

Code 11: *For Technological Evolution*: Develop technologies to strengthen and expand the voices of caring and reason and the abundance of life, rather than technologies that ever more powerfully threaten to, and indeed then are driven to, launch and kill life

✷

Moral Evolution. "Living by the Golden Rule" is the indicator of progression. "Power of greed and corruption" is the indicator of regression. The indicator of progression for the Measure becomes this statement for the Code:

Code 12: *For Moral Evolution*: Differently stated but the same for all, the message of thousands of studies of progressive science is exactly the same as for thousands of years for progressive religion: Do unto others as ye would have them do unto you—rather than do it unto others before they can do it unto you.

MEASURING EVOLUTION

✷

Spiritual Evolution. "Sense of identity with humanity and greater being" is the indicator of progression. "Slavery to materiality" is the indicator of regression. The indicator of progression for the Measure becomes this statement for the Code:

Code 13: *For Spiritual Evolution*: Affirm our identity but also our responsibility in tandem with a greater being, a greater reality, or a greater mission, rather than fool yourself by claiming some one and only holy deity, idea, or cause for your own low ends.

✷

The Evolution of Consciousness. "Cognitive, affective, and conative scope" is the indicator of progression. "Curtailing of scope of mind" is the indicator of regression. The indicator of progression for the Measure becomes this statement for the Code:

Code 14: *For the Evolution of Consciousness*: The most precious gift of evolution is consciousness. Love, nurture, and expand it, rather than automatically seek to narrow, blunt, or otherwise slap it into shape and seize the pitiful remnant for your own low ends.

✷

ACTION. "Encouragement of progressive social action" is the indicator of progression. "Repression of progressive social action" is the indicator of regression. The indicator of progression for the Measure becomes this statement for the Code:

Code 15: *For the Evolution of Action*: For over 100,000 years the choice before our species has been unchanging. Either join those who take action on behalf of the better world, or fall back in shame or ignorance with those willing to sell out to the highest bidder and join the march to extinction.

III. *The Moral Reckoning:*
Results of the Pilot Study of G.W.Bush Presidential and Republican Congressional Majority Policies

Cosmic Evolution. As countless actions have made evident, Bush administration policies of "opposition to environmental action and global concern" are an active expression of the Global Sounding indicator of evolutionary *regression* "environmental devastation." *This clearly violates Global Sounding Moral Code 1.*

Chemical Evolution. Policies of "opposition to environmental action and global concern" are again an active expression of the evolutionary *regression* indicator "environmental devastation." *This clearly violates Global Sounding Moral Code 2.*

Biological Evolution. Again, policies of "opposition to environmental action and global concern" are an active expression of the evolutionary *regression* indicator "environmental devastation." *This clearly violates Global Sounding Moral Code 3.*

Evolution of the Brain. Policies to "minimize governmental support for nutrition and love" are an active expression of the evolutionary *regression* indicator "lack of love and nutrition." Violates Global Sounding Moral Code 4.

Psychological Evolution. Policies to "maximize defense, minimize growth motivation" are an active expression of the evolutionary *regression* indicator "lack of fulfillment." Violates Global Sounding Moral Code 5.

Cultural Evolution. Policies to "minimize support for the arts" are an active expression of the evolutionary *regression* indicator "low priority for arts." Violates Global Sounding Moral Code 6. (See End Document "The Problem of a Single Indicator for Cultural Evolution" in *Measuring Evolution).*

Social Evolution. Policies to "maximize control and inequality" are an active expression of the evolutionary *regression* indicator "control and inequality." Violates Global Sounding Moral Code 7.

Economic Evolution. Policies to "maximize imbalance through privatization" are an active expression of the evolutionary *regression* indicator "imbalanced private/public." Violates Global Sounding Moral Code 8.

Political Evolution. Policies favoring the stealthy advance of an "oligarchic probe toward fascism" are an active expression of the evolutionary *regression* indicator "authoritarianism." Violates Global Sounding Moral Code 9.

Educational Evolution. Policies to accelerate a "radical de-escalation for progressive education" are an active expression of the evolutionary *regression* indicator "curtailing of facilities for learning and independent thinking." Violates Global Sounding Moral Code 10.

Technological Evolution. Policies to support "radical escalation for the military and technologies of destruction" are an active expression of the evolutionary *regression* indicator "emphasis on technologies of destruction." Violates Global Sounding Moral Code 11.

Moral Evolution. In contrast to "Living by the Golden Rule," stances and policies for "Living by the Brass Rule" are an active expression of the evolutionary *regression* indicator "power of greed and corruption." Violates Global Sounding Moral Code 12.

Spiritual Evolution. Stances and policies to prioritize the "celebration of the absolute power of wealth" are an active expression of the evolutionary *regression* indicator "slavery to materiality." Violates Global Sounding Moral Code 13.

Evolution of Consciousness. Stances, policies, and actions designed to play to the anti-intellectualism of the masses, and to numb, dumb down, and revel in "devaluing the scope of mind" are an active expression of the evolutionary *regression* indicator "curtailing of the scope of mind." Violates Global Sounding Moral Code 14.

ACTION. Stances and policies to advocate, fund, and dictate "encouragement of regressive social action" are an active expression of the evolutionary *regression* indicator "repression of progressive social action." Violates Global Sounding Moral Code 15.

A BRIEF, INFORMAL HISTORY OF MEASURES OF GLOBAL WELL-BEING

A vast amount of work—too much of which is being forgotten, but which increasingly calls for wider recognition among scientists and global policy and decision makers—has gone into the development of scientific measures of global well-being.

This document is written to celebrate and indicate the scope of this work and its relevance to the development of the Global Sounding, which otherwise might seem to be only an unintelligible upstart out of nowhere.

We'll briefly summarize some of this work under the following categories: Social science pioneers. Futurist movement. Evolutionary systems science movement. Human potentials movement. Quality of Life and local and global Well-Being movements. Women's movement. Psychiatric measures. Moral measures. Spiritual measures. Action context.

Because of the huge number of references this document would require, and because practically all are quickly accessible today via Google or other excellent internet search engine, we will only provide the names for search engines here, with list of references for later editions.

DAVID LOYE

Social Science Pioneers

The earliest impactful work was that of a group of brilliant psychologists roughly publishing from 1940 into the 1980s. Motivated by post-World War II concern about the continuing threat of fascism in American and well as other national contexts was the work of Adorno, Frenkel-Brunswick, Levinson, and Sanford in development of the F Scale to identify the characteristics of the "authoritarian personality" versus the "democratic personality." This specific aim was expanded into the development of measures for multi-level, cross-cultural studies of human values by Milton Rokeach, by Charles Osgood of the semantic differential measuring differences in meaning, and David McClelland of the drive of need-for-achievement in gaining global economic well-being.

Two notable pioneers in the development of opinion polling—since proved to be probably the single most progressively impactful social scientific invention—were George Gallup and Hadley Cantril. Both were originally associated with the pioneering opinion polling center at Princeton University. A short essay by Cantril, "The Human Design," is one of the best statements I ever saw of what constitutes the ideal for the good person and good society.

Also at Princeton was the great psychologist Silvan Tomkins, considered a genius within the field in his time. Tomkins' studies established a scientific vocabulary for identifying emotional similarities and differences cross-culturally, and a script theory for exploring the universality of stories in the construction of lives and personalities.

Global Sounding Relevance: The Global Sounding is similar to

Adorno and others in using a scale of indicators. It is different, however, in providing a much shorter list of indicators with wider scope through its multidisciplinary orientation to levels and activities of evolution. It is designed with the potential to find a place both in polling and in multi-level education. As a matter of personal involvement, I was the senior author with Milton Rokeach of the section on some of this work "Ideology, Belief Systems, Values, and Attitudes" in the *International Encyclopedia of Neurology, Psychiatry, Psychoanalysis and Psychology*. Tomkins, whose work I wrote of in *The Healing of a Nation* and *The Leadership Passion*, was a close friend while I lived in Princeton, worked at the Educational Testing Service, and briefly taught at the University.

Futurist Movement

Aimed specifically at building the better global future, launched during the 1960s by Bertrand de Jouvenel in France and others in Europe and the U.S., the futurist movement produced a dramatic advance in global measurements. The best known of these advances were the early studies of the Club of Rome financed by highly practical business and industrial visionaries, who saw the writing on the wall if the world did not wake up to where we were headed and—of critical importance—had the money to do something about it.

The first Club of Rome study to seize world headlines was Limits to Growth. Using the powerful new tool of computer modeling based on the work of Jay Forrester and others at MIT in Systems Dynamics, Donella and Dennis Meadows and Jorgen Randers were able to show that unless we radically changed our ways all life on this planet—including us—was headed for disaster. Besides awakening the world to this threat, the goal for their study was "a model that represents a world system that is: "sustainable without sudden and uncontrollable collapse, and capable of satisfying the basic material requirements of all of its people."

This first study of the "outer limits to growth" was followed by a Club of Rome study of the "inner limits to growth" by systems philosopher, futurist, and general evolution theorist Ervin Laszlo. Out of this came the voluminous *Goals for Mankind*—which began to shape United Nations' measurement development as Laszlo became full time involved with the UN—charting the goals and values of people, nations, and organizations to determine what we have in common to lay the foundations for a better future, rather than merely cycling in place or regressing backward.

In tune with this thrust was the development of other measures, such as Olaf Helmer's Delphi method of obtaining expert consensus, Kenneth and Elise Boulding's exploration of the universal impact of the images that shape our goals, and more recently the work of Aleco Christakis and Ken Bausch. An original member of the Club of Rome creative team, Christakis has persisted in developing new computerized methods of gaining consensus in cross-cultural situations of the conflict between people and organizations with widely differing goals and perceptions of one another.

Global Sounding Relevance: The Global Sounding takes into account the perspectives of both the "outer" and the "inner" limits to growth studies, with indicators based either on a prevailing consensus among scientists or my guess as to the probable consensus given another decade or so for a worsening of our planetary situation to force consensus. Again, the Global Sounding has the advantage of going for the widest possible scope with a short scale with minimal indicators. Laszlo, Christakis, and Bausch are members of the Council of The Darwin Project, which I founded in 2003. As a further matter of personal involvement, I wrote of this area of studies and measures in *The Knowable Future* and developed a number of original measures for exploring key factors here—e.g., the Moral Sensitivity Profile (MSP), the Psychic Sensitivity Profile (PSP), Ideological Matrix Prediction (IMP), with development and results reported in *The Knowable Future*, and the Hemispheric Consensus Prediction (HCP), with development reported in *The Sphinx and the Rainbow* and *An Arrow Through Chaos*.

Evolutionary Systems Science Movement

Closely allied to the futurist movement was the development of the evolutionary systems science movement. The fundamental importance of this movement within this picture of the development of global measures of well-being is that it radically advanced the scientific grounding for goals and methods by providing the beginning for an adequate matrix or "home" within an action-oriented theory of evolution.

Beginning with Ludwig von Bertelanffy in biology, this new perspective first surfaced within the development of general systems theory (GST). As was understable in getting underway within the opposition of rigidly departmentalized mainstream science, GST tended to study systems in present time alignments. But out of the perception that no system could be adequately understood or dealt with without attention to the dimension of time—or evolutionary movement from past, to present, to future—the expanded perspective of *evolutionary* systems science gradually took form in a striking modern revival of a "controversial" philosophy with tenacious ancient roots.

First taking form in the philosophy of Aristotle in ancient Greece and development of the I Ching guide to enlightened leadership in ancient China, this was the dialectical perspective of movement through time that became verboten with reaction to the emphasis of Marx and Engels on dialectical thinking and action. Rising again in the 20th century within nonpolitical contexts, however—and avoiding the old root word "dialectical"—this became the new thrust for the general and computer model exploration of cybernetic, chaos, and complexity theories. Among those advancing this modern explosion of evolutionary systems scientific theories were Kurt Lewin in psychology, Kenneth Boulding in economics and sociology, C.West Churchman in moral alignment, Alexander Luria and Karl Pribram in brain research, Mihaly Csikzsentmihalyi with his concept of "flow," and again Ervin Laszlo in the articulation of a time- and action-driven general systems theory.

Key moves in the development of this perspective were the formation of the General Evolution Research Group by Laszlo and others including myself, The Washington Society for Evolution Studies, the Society for Chaos Theory in Psychology and the Life Sciences, of which I was a co-founder, the Darwin Project, of which I was the founder, and other work involving members of the multinational, multidisciplinary International Society for Systems Science (ISSS).

Global Sounding Relevance: The two key developments leading to the development of the Global Sounding were the formation of the General Evolution Research Group and the Darwin Project. Laszlo, Karl Pribram and Mihaly Csikzsentmihalyi are members of both GERG and the Council of The Darwin Project. Two books articulating the grounding scientific and educational perspective by members of the General Evolution Research Group and The Darwin Project Council are *The Great Adventure: Toward a Fully Human Theory of Evolution* and *The Evolutionary Outrider: The Impact of the Human Agent on Evolution*. My book *Darwin's Lost Theory* shows the grounding of this "full spectrum," moral- and action-oriented perspective in Darwin.

Human Potentials Movement

Historically, one of the most important shifts within science toward measures of global well-being came about through a trend within prior thought given a globally impactful and measurement-oriented voice by psychologist Abraham Maslow. Pointing to the inadequacy of the prevailing psychology of pathology, Maslow not only called for but spelled out the nature of what was needed for a psychology of well-being in 1948. This helped launch an international flood of new therapies for what came to be called the Human Potentials Movement and the new fields of humanistic psychology, transpersonal psychology, and—and currently highly creative—positive psychology.

Since 1961 the main organization at the core of this development has been the Association for Humanistic Psychology. In 1964 a conference at old Saybrook in Connecticut—bringing together Gordon Allport, J.F.T. Bugental, Charlotte Buhler, Rollo May, Gardner Murphy, Henry Murray, Carl Rogers, and Maslow—further spelled out and shaped the future for the movement. This led to the formation of Saybrook Graduate School and Research Center in San Francisco. Since 1975 Saybrook has focused on the development of a humanistic systems science and the practicalities of a humanistic management science—vital for the kind of training and influence on leadership in business and government for which the current world situation events display such global need.

Over the years humanistic psychologists have developed a variety of measures with impact mainly limited to the needs of new methods of therapy and business and governmental management. Currently, however, as a reflection let us hope of the influence of an aroused Global Mind, this body of work is finding a significant relevance in its resonation to the vision of a measure of Gross National Happiness, or GNH, aimed at going far beyond the old Gross National Product, or GNP, for assessing global well-being.

Originally the idea in 1972 of a 17-year-old boy on becoming King of Bhutan—seemingly naive at the time, but since then, as the world situation has worsened, looking increasingly practical—the idea of the GNH is being given serious consideration by international conferences of economists and others trying to figure out how, out of the present mess, to build a better world. A fascinating factor here is the fact that Bhutan is a remote and tiny country high in the Himalayas sandwiched between China and India. For many this calls to mind the *Lost Horizon* vision of Shangri-La, also particularly appealing for many is the GNH's reflection of the Buddhist vision of basic requirements for moral as well as general evolution.

Global Sounding Relevance. The considerable influence of humanistic psychology and the human potentials movement on and relevance to the development of the Global Sounding can be seen in the specific wording for all of its indicators on up from the evolution of the brain—that is, indicators, both plus and minus, for psychological, social, cultural, educational, economic, political, technical, moral and spiritual evolution, and the evolution of consciousness and social action. GERG and Darwin Project Council members include Stanley Krippner, a formative figure and former president of the Association for Humanistic Psychology, and Mihaly Csikszentmihalyi, formative in the development of positive psychology. Krippner and GERG and Darwin Project Council member Allan Combs are Saybrook Graduate School faculty members. With a foreword by Csikszentmihalyi, our SUNY Press text *The Great Adventure: Toward a Fully Human Theory of Evolution* includes chapters by Combs, myself, and GERG co-founder and Darwin Project Council member Riane Eisler—whose cultural evolution theory has influenced the development of the work of many humanistic psychologists during recent years. I am on the editorial council for the journal *Advanced Development* and have frequently written of the work of Maslow and others in my books and in journals. Of particularly fascinating serendipity in relation to Bhutan, the GNH, and the Shangri La vision, originally written many years back from now, is my forthcoming book *The Parable of the Three Villages*.

Quality of Life Indicators and Local and Global Measures of Wellbeing Movements

In many ways the goals for much of this earlier and contemporary work are being reached through the remarkable proliferation of the

DAVID LOYE

Quality of Life Indicators and Local and Global Measures of Wellbeing movements over the past two decades. Because of their sharing of perspectives, techniques, and people we're considering them together here.

A powerfully impactful development of measures of global wellbeing has been the boom in Quality of Life indicators. Likely the most influential and widely used is the United Nations Human Development Index (HDI), produced by the UN Development Programme every year since 1990. The HDI began by weighting per capita income, education, and life expectancy to produce a rank for every one of the 190 member countries of the United Nations. In 2002 HDI expanded to focus on Deepening Democracy in a Fragmented World, and in 2003 to focus on Millennium Development Goals, which commits the member states of the United Nations to cut poverty and increase funding for health and education.

The other current major measure is the Calvert-Henderson Quality of Life Indicators. Launched by crusading futurist economist Hazel Henderson and a leader in the field of responsible social investing, the Calvert Fund, Calvert-Henderson measures the degree to which we are moving ahead or not in education, employment, energy, environment, health, human rights, income, infrastructure, national security, public safety, re-creation and shelter. Based on Henderson's original global systems analysis, this measure has behind it 25 years of research and advocacy worldwide for something better than the ubiquitous—and grievously inadequate—Gross National Product, or GNP, to monitor global development.

A study of indicators particularly important in exploring the link of gender equality to global advancement for all humanity is "Women,

MEASURING EVOLUTION

Men, and the Global Quality of Life," about which we'll have more to say in the next section on measures and the women's movement.

Some other indicators of the rapid spread and power of this perspective on measures of global well-being are these: The new UK Government Sustainable Development Strategy, Securing the Future, launched by Prime Minister Tony Blair in 2005. The Big Cities Quality of Life Report for conditions in New Zealand's eight largest cities, launched in 1999. The Canadian Policy Research Networks (CPRN), aimed at the development of a Quality of Life measure, has completed a series of dialogues on quality of life with Canadians from all walks of life, coast to coast. Greater Phoenix, Arizona, and Carver County, Maryland, have Qualify of Life Indicators. Sustainable Seattle, with a 99 indicator measure heavily involving community involvement, claims theirs is a "powerful program, run on a shoestring," which "could be done by any community."

Comments Limits to Growth co-author Donella Meadows: "The idea of citizens choosing their own indicators is something new under the sun—something intensely democratic."

Sharing many of the same goals, techniques, and experts with the Quality of Life Indicator movement is the local and global Wellbeing movement. An example of the scope but also the complexity of the instruments for both movements is the description provided by Robert Prescott-Allen in *The Wellbeing of Nations* (Island Press, 2001). 36 indicators of health, population, wealth, education, communication, freedom, peace, crime, and equity for a Human Wellbeing Index are combined with 51 indicators of land health, protected areas, water quality, water supply, global atmosphere, air quality, species diversity, energy use, and resource pressures into an Ecosystem Wellbeing Index.

DAVID LOYE

Another characteristic of Wellbeing measures is to go beyond the statistics of such objective indicators to also get at subjective indicators, or how people feel about their lives or what is happening to them. Are they happy, which can prevail in seemingly bad circumstances, or miserable, which can prevail in seemingly the wealthiest and supposedly advanced circumstances. Here an important factor has been the interest of Asian countries in developing measures better tailored to their regional development than standard Western measures. The AustralianUnity Wellbeing Index is an example. Sparked by interest in Hong Kong, Taiwan and Singapore, currently most promising is the formation in 2001 of an International Wellbeing Group. Under the leadership of Professor Robert Cummins from the Australian Centre on Quality of life development of an International Wellbeing Index involves 80 researchers from 40 countries. Also notable in this picture is the Living Planet Index developed by the World Wildlife Fund (WWF).

A particularly colorful and intriguing development for the Wellbeing measures movement is reported in the new book *Child Honoring: How To Turn This World Around* (Praeger, 2006). A chapter by none other than Ronald Colman (not the long gone famous star of the classic wellbeing movie Lost Horizon, of course, but rather now the head of the Canadian wellbeing research group GPI Atlantic) tells of work to develop a new Canadian Index of Wellbeing. The interesting new edge to its perspective is measurement of the prime factors for "creating a society that genuinely honours its children, one that would leave them a liveable world to inherit."

A key inspiration for the measure is the world-famous Canadian "children's troubadour" Raffi, editor of *Child Honoring* and passionate

MEASURING EVOLUTION

promoter of the new measure. One of the most vital goals for all of these measures, Quality of Life as well as Wellbeing, is to offset or replace the present overwhelming reliance by economists, businesses and government on the deeply entrenched gross inadequacies of the GDP, or Gross Domestic Product. To provide the Wellbeing measurement movement with a song to grab global attention, Raffi has written and performs "Count With Me"—with a premiere performance backed by a chorus of economists appropriately dubbed "The Indicators."

Global Sounding Relevance: Developed not to replace but rather to augment these measures, the Global Sounding obviously differs considerably from all of them in going for the same ends with a much shorter and simpler set of indicators. At the same time it notably shares the goal of measuring subjective as well as objective factors, indeed in some ways it is a unique blend of both approaches. Most importantly—and for this reason I hope it may find use within both of these movements—its fifteen positive and fifteen negative indicators provide a new measurable plus/minus perspective on both Quality of Life and Wellbeing indicators within a "fully human" evolutionary perspective.

Of personal relevance, cultural evolution theorist Riane Eisler and I are currently involved in developing a Caring Economics Index to accompany publication of a new book she is finishing. Hazel Henderson is a much admired old friend, member of the Darwin Project Council, and author of a chapter in *The Evolutionary Outrider.* Along with Henderson's forceful early projection, in 1971 I was a pioneer in developing a scientific methodology for applying the idea of the "electronic town meeting" to gaining consensus on social advancement indicators in *The Healing of a Nation.* Similarly, Raffi is a much treasured close friend and also a member of the Darwin Project Council.

It is admiration of people like these that keeps one going.

The Women's Movement

The ideal for test development is maximum validity and reliability with a minimal number of questions. In other words, the ideal measure of global well-being would consist of only a single question that cut through all surfaces to tap a single factor accounting for the widest possible range of positive or negative effects.

Is such a thing possible? In the 19th century social utopian Charles Fourier was possibly the first to flatly state that all future social progress would occur "in proportion to the advance of women toward liberty." As with the case of the 17-year-old Bhutan King, here is another idea for a long time considered naive now being seriously pursued by a wide range of measurement developers.

With possibly the greatest potential impact are two new measures for the universally well-established and widely respected United Nation Development reports, or UNDP. The Gender-related Development Index, or GDI, has three indicators (relative life expectancy, relative education, and proportion of earned income). The Gender Empowerment Measure, or GEM, has three more (proportion of women in parliament, proportion in top jobs, and female share of earned income).

This, however, is only the ubiquitous tip of the iceberg. The Minimum Development Goals for the United Nations—which the Bush

MEASURING EVOLUTION

presidency in America did everything it possibly could to gut and undermine—include the promotion of gender equality and the empowering of women. Since 1985 in Nairobi and again in 1995 in Beijing, the huge UN Decade for Women conferences have focused on the need for measures proving the link between gender equality and global well-being. Since 1998 the European Union has been working to develop a good set of indicators of gender equality for developed countries. Since 2002, Spanish, Danish, Irish, Dutch, and Greek presidencies have been developing measures of indicators of violence against women.

The Gender Gap Report quantifies the size of the gender gap in 58 countries, including all 30 OECD countries and 28 other emerging markets.

Since 1972 the Global Health Council has been pushing in this direction. In 1993—in the rather astounding consensus for 100 leaders of all major world faiths obtained by theologian Hans Kung—the World Parliament of Religions included an equal partnership between women and men as a fundamental plank in Kung's powerful statement of a Global Ethic.

Mindful of much of this, in 1995 a small American nonprofit institute, in a report "Women, Men, and the Global Quality of Life," hit the nail on the head, one might say. Setting out to "test the hypothesis that gender equity is strongly related to quality of life throughout the world," the three main researchers involved pulled together a vast range of data on 89 nations, or a majority of the countries of the world. Sources included the UN Development Reports and both GNP and G.P., or Gross Domestic Project. This data was then used to explore "the relation between . . .gender equity and quality of life variables" with the heavy weight scientific and statistical methodology of "descriptive, correlational, factor, and multiple regression analyses."

The result was that "the hypothesized link . . . was confirmed at a very high level of statistical significance for correlational analysis . . . further confirmed by factor analysis" . . . with regression analysis also yielding "significant results."

"An R-square of .84, with statistical significance at the .0001 level, provides support for the hypothesis that gender equity is a strong indicator of the quality of life."

Global Sounding Relevance. I'm understandably, I should think, delighted to report that the small nonprofit was the Center for Partnership Studies, co-founded by cultural evolution theorist Riane Eisler and myself. The principal instigator, investigator, and author for the report was Eisler, with myself and our intern young sociologist Kari Norgaard as co-investigators and authors. Besides CPS board members, among those to be thanked for support with funds for this project, as well as the basic support for CPS that made it possible, were the Roy A. Hunt Foundation, The Threshold Foundation, The Laurence Rockefeller Foundation, The Epstein Family Foundation, the Shaler-Adams Foundation, and the Seven Springs Foundation.

Psychiatric Measures

As noted in the section of this book on the first use of the Global Sounding in a pilot test of Bush era policies, an important precursor for development of the Global Sounding was the Minnesota Multiphasic Personality Inventory. Generally known as the MMPI, this is a test widely used by therapists and in personnel management for measuring degrees of personal and social maladjustments in terms of indicators such as ego inflation, hypomanic activation, bizarre mentation, interpersonal suspiciousness, amorality, and similar scales.

As one might guess, by now the MMPI is only one of many comparable measures that, while designed to measure individual pathology, through their standardized worldwide use can also, by focusing on the leaders and followers involved, provide a valid glimpse into potentially positive or negative impacts of policies, projects, movements, or beliefs on global health and well-being.

In universal use, for example, is *The Handbook of Psychiatric Measures* published by the American Psychiatric Association, with over 900 pages of measures and an accompanying CD-ROM providing complete copies of 108 of these measures. Another source in worldwide use by psychiatrists and psychologists is the DSM, or *Diagnostic and Statistical Manual of Mental Disorders*. Typical of a trend toward use of psychiatric measures to go beyond individual to assessment of group and global well-being is still another book, *Quality of Life and Pharmacoeconomics in Clinical Trials*, which includes chapters on measures of quality of life for specific conditions including cross-cultural issues and assessment in disadvantaged groups.

Global Sounding Relevance. An important study for my purposes was carried out in Israel comparing results on a selection of comparable indicators for the MMPI with two other leading personality inventories, the Comrey and Eysenck Personality Scales. It found comparable validities for the three—in other words, results for use of any one of them were reasonably backed up by the others.

DAVID LOYE

While on the faculty of the UCLA School of Medicine, as Research Director for the project over more than half a decade, I included the Comrey measure in a large battery of tests including the Rokeach values measure, measures of sensitivity to gender relations, and my own original measures of moral sensitivity and other qualities in a pioneering study of the impact of movies and television on adults of diverse ages, gender, and ideology. Since then, in a study I report in my forthcoming book *Making It in the Dream Factory*, I have continued to explore the multi-variable impact of movies and television on human evolution. Chapter ten of *Bankrolling Evolution,* The Madness of Kings and the Case for Revolution, in the case of the G.W.Bush presidency, Congress, and support among voters also explores the relevance of psychiatric factors to global well-being.

Again, behind indicators from the evolution of the brain on up, can be seen the influence of this experiential background on the development of the Global Sounding.

Moral Measures

Other than among specialists, the only reasonably well-known measure of moral evolution is the Kohlberg Moral Development Scale. Developed by Harvard psychologist Lawrence Kohlberg, this measure of seven stages of moral development was the first to gain testing and worldwide use in cross-cultural comparisons.

Prior to Kohlberg, however, there were major studies and lesser known measures of moral development with speculative world relevance by psychologists J.M.Baldwin and Jean Piaget. Moreover, since Kohlberg's tragic death in 1987 ventures in this direction have mushroomed. Among measures influenced by or developed by Kohlberg's research assistants are the Defining Issues Test, the Moral Judgement Interview, the Social Reflection Questionnaire, and the Moral Judgement Test. Another measure in reasonably wide use is the Values and Behavior Survey of the Joseph and Edna Josephson Institute of Values. Earlier mentioned was Milton Rokeach's classic Rokeach Values Scale.

The most comprehensive—and frankly astounding—measure is the World Values Survey (www.worldvaluessurvey.org). Advanced by an international network of social scientists, under the aegis of the World Values Survey Association, chiefly funded by the Bank of Sweden Tercentenary Foundation and various scientific foundations, in four waves of worldwide testing WVS has been gathering data bearing on global moral evolution since 1981.

For an idea of how much this project has to offer the shaping of governmental and industrial policy to global moral evolution one must go to the website www.worldvaluessurvey.org—and to its new offshoot www.jdsurvey.net—as there is no quick way to summarize the multinational scope, intensity, or sophistication of this venture's data gathering and analysis.

Among published sources drawing on this huge data bank two of the most useful are Ronald Inglehart's *Modernization and Postmodernism* (Princeton University Press, 1997)—with, for example, sections on value type by age group in European countries, analysis of value change, cross-national differences in satisfaction with one's life as a whole from 1973 to 1998—and in Inglehart and Klingemann, "Genes, Culture and Happiness" (MIT Press, 2000), subjective well-being by level of economic development, and subjective well-being and democratic institutions.

Global Sounding Relevance. The Global Sounding's subjective single indicator for moral evolution cannot of course begin to match the objective and multi-perspectival subjective scope of something like the World Values Survey. On the other hand, it does offer a considerable advantage in ease of use. Bearing on this area of major personal interest, the Global Sounding also has behind it my books *The Healing of a Nation;* forthcoming *The River and the Star, The Science of Evil,* and *Making It in the Dream Factory;* and my development of ad hoc measures of moral sensitivity for various research projects, including development of quite possibly the first scientifically grounded Global Ethic for reporting in *The Glacier and the Flame.*

Spiritual Measures

For thousands of years religions have been the chief generators of measures of spiritual and moral evolution. Two of many instances, for example, are the Ten Commandments for Christians and Jews and the Eightfold Path for Buddhism.

To this venture science is very much a johnny-come-lately. However, in this area the great excitement for our time is the potential liberation of new ways of shaping and updating the best of the old measures to the increasingly grave challenges of the 21st century. That is, through a new wedding of progressive science with progression religion, the goal is liberation from the persisting holy wars and the creation of hell rather than heaven on earth by regression religions that, along with regressive science, presently drive our species toward

MEASURING EVOLUTION

destruction.

For many the most impactful step for the 20th century in this new direction was the pioneering wedding of science and religion in the evolutionary vision of anthropologist and renegade Catholic priest Pierre de Chardin (1881-1955).

Of many milestones since then among the most important have been the eruption out of Western science of the morally and spiritually-oriented moves toward measurement of some of the pioneers in the formation of what became humanistic psychology, such as Maslow, Roberto Assaggioli, Kazamierz Dabrowski. In contrast, originally out of a grounding orientation to Eastern philosophy and spirituality—and the greater sophistication of the Eastern understanding of the responsibilities of our relation to evolution—came the integrating work and impact of the brilliant and controversial "New Age" philosopher Ken Wilber.

A particularly powerful and increasingly popular wedding of progressive science with progressive religion has been the development by Clare Graves and Don Beck of the spiral dynamics perspective. Resonating to both of these approaches, but adding the drive of a particularly appealing creative visionary, is Barbara Marx Hubbard's wide-ranging experimental exploring of new ways for people to work together in conscious evolution. Articulating the vital relation of politics to spiritual as well as moral evolution is the work of psychologist and Rabbi Michael Lerner.

Collectively, the Wilber, Beck, Hubbard, and Lerner ventures contain a rich and vibrant source of possibilities for the development of global measures of well-being. Quite possibly farthest along in this direction is the Wilber-Combs Lattice developed by Wilber and psychologist and evolutionary systems scientist Allan Combs. At present, however, the greatest single advance in this direction has been theologian Hans Kung's updating of ancient measures in development of a multinational, multicultural, and multispiritual Global Ethic.

Also farther along from the viewpoint of the standardizing of formal measures of spiritual evolution—i.e., pummeling the hell out of them with the statistical analyses needed to establish validity and reliability—seem to be a handful of more conventional measures. Of these, the Spiritual Involvement and Beliefs Scale (SIBS) is said to have advantages over others with broader scope, terms transcending cultural-religious bias, and assessment of both beliefs and actions. The Spiritual Well-Being Scale (SWBS) is widely used. Still another measure, The Spiritual Evolution Assessment Scale (SEAS), is being developed by the School for Esoteric Studies.

Global Sounding Relevance. In contrast to the vast spread and complexity of all of the above, the Global Sounding selection of two indicators (plus and minus) for spiritual evolution will seem not only naive but beyond belief jutzpah and heresy to many test-development methodologists. I would be willing to bet, however, that bundling them in with a multiplicity of items from the above measures for factor analysis would find them high on the resulting prime factor.

The main thing to keep in mind from the measurement viewpoint is that in its simple, intuitively validating directness, this is a particularly bold venture moving beyond the box of science into the grand but practical mystery of spirituality.

Of the above named venturers the following are members of the Darwin Project Council (with relevant books here in parentheses: Hans

MEASURING EVOLUTION

Kung *(A Global Ethic)*. Allan Combs *(The Radiance of Being)*. Michael Lerner *(The Left Hand of God)*. Barbara Marx Hubbard *(Conscious Evolution)*. Riane Eisler *(Sacred Pleasure)*. And myself *(The Glacier and the Flame, The Parable of the Three Villages, The Science of Evil)*.

Action Context

All of these categories for measures of global well-being—as well as the science, education, and the societies behind them—have been, and are, driven ahead by the caring, the nurturance, and the inspiration as well as the poking, prodding, and general hell-raising of the activists of progressive science, progressive religion, and progressive leadership in all fields.

As historically and currently revealed by the book out of which *Measuring Evolution* emerged, *Bankrolling Evolution,* this progressive forward thrust for humanity has been—and is—blocked, ignored, downgraded or diverted by a functionally sub-human mass hitched to us like a ball and chain.

Alternately heavier or lighter, the drag of this ball on human evolution is composed of fellow beings who do look very much like all the rest of us, and with all of whom we have much in common, but with this critical difference. They're either blindly content with whatever happens to be the prevailing status quo, or they're cowed into submission by the leadership of those who through greed for power and both personal and mass pathology would drive us backward in evolution.

The science of every field now tells us we've run out of time for fence-straddling or floating indecisively in-between these two basic alignments. We either join the humans, and the action tradition for all the fields surveyed here, and fight for the better world—or see our world fitfully roll backward into nowhere with the sub-human ball and chain.

Global Sounding Relevance. Of all the measures here surveyed, the Global Sounding is the first measure I know of to make action the driving edge, culmination, and valued top of the tree of evolution.

This, above all, was the creed for all the great minds before us and is the creed for all those living to whom the present and future development of the Global Sounding is dedicated.

THE SCIENTIFIC AND POLITICAL GROUNDING FOR THE SOUNDING

To make clear what was otherwise by necessity cryptic in the matrix for the Global Sounding measure, here—moving along the established progression for evolution from "bottom" to "top"—is a brief explanation for each level not only in terms of evolutionary systems science.

Of most importance is what, in terms of a smattering of history, these brief descriptions for each level indicate is happening to the America of Washington, Jefferson, and Franklin, with devastating ripple effects rolling out through our world today.

This essentially duplicates chapter fourteen for *Bankrolling Evolution*.

Cosmic evolution

The multi-billion year progression from the hypothetical Big Bang, to the evolutionary formation of planets, to the emergence of ours as the only place we know of in the universe capable of supporting life indicates how precious is the living environment in all aspects to us, as well as to whatever meaning there might exist beyond us.

The opposition to environmental action and colossal indifference to global concern of the Regression Syndrome is worldwide probably most widely seen as the source of its single most consistently horrifying acts.

Chemical evolution . . .

. . . emerges out of the processes most easily visualized as the interplay of what is known as symbiosis with natural selection, within the liquid living environment of the Gaian "soup"—which hypothetically interconnects all life according to the Gaian hypothesis of astrophysicist James Lovelock and biologist Lynn Margulis. Among others, this level of evolution was intimately explored by the late Nobel Laureate Ilya Prigogine, author with Isabelle Stengers of *Order Out of Chaos* and an honorary member of our General Evolution Research Group.

Here again the Regression Syndrome's opposition to environmental action and indifference to global concern is an astonishment for the onset of the 21st century.

Biological evolution . . .

. . . can be measured in many ways. A vital indicator at the level of emergence for our species is the degree of health and longevity the people of this earth as a whole have attained and can maintain. *This in turn is dependent on the degree to which the food we eat, the water we drink, and the air we breath is life-giving rather than life-depleting or life-destroying.*

Here even more than ever—as it directly involves us and our children and whatever life future generations are to enjoy—the sellout to corporate interests behind opposition to environmental action is the blackest of black marks for the Regression Syndrome.

The Launch Point for "Higher Evolution"

Our brains, emerging at the dividing line between the lower and the higher levels of evolution, each contain—in the swelling upward from the top of the spinal column to the cerebrum and frontal brain—the amazing record of evolution from origins billions of years ago into now, possibly even foreshadowing the destiny of species.

Much research shows us that the development of the neuronal networks of which our brains are composed are heavily dependent on the amount and kind of love as well as nutrition the brains of each of us receive during our earliest years.

The fact that every year on this earth 3 million children die of AIDS and about 11 million children die of preventable causes "often for want of simple and easily provided improvements in nutrition, sanitation, and maternal health and education" (Human Development Report 2002) indicates how great is the gap between the need and the deadly drum beat of multi-billion-dollar tax cuts shoved through a supine U.S.Congress by the Regression Machine.

Tax cuts, one must note, that are decried by all but the most suborned of economists as mainly serving the incredibly wealthy few in America, while under-cutting the future for our species by gutting services not only benefitting the brains and bodies of the many in America but also all those worldwide who used to look to America for hope and leadership.

DAVID LOYE

Steps Toward the Better Future

Psychological or personal evolution, as earlier indicated, is perhaps most easily captured in terms of the work of the pioneering humanistic psychologist Abraham Maslow.

In identifying the characteristics of the *self-actualizer* Maslow seems to have gone a long way toward capturing the evolutionary ideal for our species. Central for Maslow was the picture of our evolutionary development as a progression from *defense* of our self and our own turf as our basic motivation, to the motivational liberation of the *growth* of sensitivity to the needs of others as well as ourselves, to ultimately the drive of a level of *metamotivation* as the highest reach for our consciousness.

As for the Regression Syndrome, in everything from its traditionally relentless search for The Enemy (communists, liberals, feminists, environmentalists, secular humanists, democrats, et cetera), to the psychosocial blind-siding of growth and metamotivation to relentlessly shift ever larger funds from the technologies of peace to the military, it maximizes a fixation on *defense* as the only proper level of mind and motivation for the proper American—and for America's proper client, customer, or servant population to empire elsewhere.

Cultural evolution, long recognized by the expert but disregarded by biological extremists and the masses as the *sine qua non* for human evolution, is actually the broad category containing all levels and activities above it on the charted "tree of evolution."

It is bracketed in the Global Sounding matrix to indicate the narrow but vital sub-category for our customary association of the word culture with the arts—that is, the writing of great books, poems and plays, as well as the composing of great music and the painting of great pictures and all else of this nature expanding our sense of life at its highest, most ecstatic or deeply meaningful.

Notably distinguishing all the great as well as the near-great periods of history, in Greece, in the Italy of Rome and the Renaissance—as well as the years of FDR's New Deal investment in art to lift the spirits of a people dragging through the Great Depression—this glory of the past for the world and for America stands today in marked contrast to the avowed priorities and goals for the "new America."

Particularly revealing is how counter to the ageold passion for *conservative* as well as progressive money for the arts and all we know as culture is the tunnel-visioned drive of the Regression Machine to subjugate the media and gut the public broadcasting system for radio and television—which currently offers us our only reliable mass contact with the greatness of the past, present, or future.

Social evolution for our species has been accelerating since the 18th century Enlightenment through the drive for greater freedom and equality against the relentless attempt of social, political, economic, and religious oligarchies and tyrannies to take over once again by reasserting the primacy of control and inequality.

Again, in policies ranging from the skillful disenfranchising of voters in key elections to the drive to roll back court protection of basic rights, the Regression Machine is clearly on the wrong side of history as well as evolution.

Economic evolution, the experience of the past 200 years by now indicates, depends on balancing the relation of the private to the public sector, as prevails in Scandinavia today—as well as, with notable lapses, has been the ideal for the U.S.

At one extreme the experience of Germany, Italy, and Japan with fascism—where industrial oligarches financed the rise of the Nazis and their Italian and Japanese equivalents as their puppets, but then found the puppet had become master—demonstrates the disaster awaiting the temporary triumph of the runaway purchase and take over of government by private enterprise. At the other extreme, communism demonstrates the disaster awaiting the triumph of the suppression of private enterprise and the attempt at regulation of all economic activity by fiat.

Oblivious to history and everything but its own insatiable need to show the world "who's boss," the Regression Machine drives relentlessly to deregulate everything from top to bottom to create the jungle for the oldest of economic and political games: the happy hunting ground for the predator as "insider," with the rest of us being relegated to the role of being his or her unsuspecting prey.

Political evolution, through thousands of years experience since the Golden Age of Greece into recent times, reveals the movement away from the authoritarian rule of the few over the many to the rule of the enlightened and the educated many over themselves.

That the Regression Machine is already well into the dynamics of oligarchy headed toward authoritarianism bodes ill for the future if successful.

Educational evolution is an obviously central but neglected marker for a species for whom evolution—contrary to the assertion of biological extremists and some so-called evolutionary psychologists—largely depends on the passage of knowledge from one generation to the next.

The fact the Regression Machine slogan of "Leave no child behind" was brazenly stolen from the Children's Defense Fund exemplifies policies designed to mask an underlying push to gut Head Start and underfund public schools to play to the Machine's funding and voting base with a shift of public funds to underwrite private and parochial schools.

Technological evolution, a critically vital level/activity for a society such as ours hopped up and almost wholly driven by it, is a tangle of wonder and horror for lack of an updated understanding. The work of cultural evolution theorist and GERG member Riane Eisler makes the vital distinction between *regressive* technologies of destruction, i.e., bigger and better bombs, and *progressive* technologies of production, reproduction, and actualization, as for example education and the techniques of the human potentials movement. In just the first two and a half years of the Regression Machine's control of all three branches of the American government the military budget went from $289 billion already bloated beyond all reason in 2000, to *$400* billion in 2003—an increase of over *$100 billion*, which alone, just the *increase,* dwarfs the military budget of every other nation on this earth.

Moral evolution has been grossly and disastrously neglected by science. In many years of study specifically of this level, concern, and, as Darwin recognized, primary function for human evolution, I have found no better measure than the indicator prevailing over thousands of years now in the progressive factions of all faiths most generally called the Golden Rule—do unto others as ye would have them do unto you.

Exemplified by the routine leadership style for relations with all others—whether those of differing race, faith, political party, class, or nationality—the inbuilt guide for the Regression Machine is the automatic display of the pious face and words to mask the practicality of the top-down operation of The Brass Rule: "Do it unto others before they can do it unto you."

Spiritual evolution is a hard level to evaluate because of the success of the strategy for the Regression Machine of expropriating God for their very own. But if one looks closely it is apparent that behind the avowed worship of God generally lies the reality of an ancient religion grounded mainly in the celebration of the absolute power of wealth.

This is evident, for example, from the prevailing evidence of a very narrow interpretation of to whom most specifically the blessings go, when from the hymnal one sings "Praise God from whom all blessings flow."

As for the *evolution of consciousness*, much is revealed by the degree to which the signaling not merely of a devaluing but even of an active contempt for intellect so often shapes off the cuff statements and policies for the Regression Machine.

This comes across most consistently in the highly practiced, generally folksy and automatic Regression Machine bid for votes or money by catering to the traditional American anti-intellectualism and widespread resentment of those labeled snobs for displaying any degree of education.

MEASURING EVOLUTION

It is policy shaped by the regressive adept and honed by the captive Ph.D. to quickly slip through the occasional window of opportunity to seize the mind of the stereotypical lesser American of beer, chips, and wall-to-wall television.

In the sharpest possible contrast, I personally, increasingly, see the evolution of consciousness as the eternal thrust within us to range out toward and gain a sense of the ultimate unity of the True, the Good, and the Beautiful, as Darwin as well as Immanuel Kant, Jesus, and other avatars were in varying ways impelled.

For *action*—to top this scale for evolutionary progression or regression—the American revolution seems to be one of the best examples of the evolutionary impact of the policy of the "encouragement of progressive social action."

Surely few could argue that the progressive social action of Franklin, Washington, Jefferson, Madison, and Hamilton—as well as of Haym Solomon and Robert Morris back then, or of Soros, Turner, Gates, and thousands of other progressive philanthropists today—has not advanced human evolution in major ways.

As for action policy for the Regression Machine, is it not precisely what the chart of the "tree of evolution" indicates?

Who, except those in one way or another on their payroll, could honestly say the regressives were and are *for,* rather than devoutly, routinely, and even ferociously *against* progressive social action from A to Z.

DAVID LOYE

Conclusion and Prognosis

It's time to wake and work on behalf of the ancient dream of the better world that is now *our* responsibility to nurture, protect, and advance.

Or in disgrace beyond expression stand by while bit by bit it is ended.

FURTHER DEVELOPMENTAL CONSIDERATIONS

The first question those well versed in the development of tests and measures will ask of a new measure is "How do we know it actually measures what it claims it can?" This is the question of validity.

The second question to be asked is "How well does it measure what it claims it can?" This is the question of reliability.

These are the vital questions for which adequate answers must be found along the way; however, as did the legendary monsters Scylla and Charybdis in the scuttling of ships in Ulysses' time, they can also serve to preserve the status quo as well as regression in science and society if wrongfully applied at the outset of development and use for new measures.

In other words, behind these two seemingly innocent questions can loom, for example, requirements for gaining the investment of sometimes immense amounts of money from generally conservative sources, as well as sometimes truly unbelievable amounts of time from hard-pressed researchers, which can either kill new measures in the cradle or delay their use for decades.

This may be hard to believe for those at the user end confronted with something of print on a few pages, which looks like something that surely couldn't have taken more than a week or two to create. I write, however, from the experience of seven years at one of the world's largest testing companies, Educational Testing Service in Princeton, monitoring the huge expenditures of time and money going into developing and updating even such wellknown American instruments as the SAT and GRE.

We will shortly return to validity and reliability. First, it is vital to understand this about the process out of which the Global Sounding emerged. The development of tests and measurements is both an art and a science. As the end document "A Brief, Informal History of Measures of Global Well-being" illustrates in the case of the Global Sounding, out of human need and science arises the need for art in the bold shaping of something new at the creative beginning. Science then takes over to test and further refine the new beginning.

This, for a familiar example, was the pattern for modern opinion polling, which began during the 1940s with the venturesome creativity of Hadley Cantril and George Gallup in Princeton. Earlier in the century this was the pattern for what eventually became the "IQ test" in all its forms. Beginning with Alfred Binet's exploration of intelligence in retarded as well as normal children, his approach was so controversial that his own scale, while gobbled up, revised, and widely applied in America as the Stanford-Binet, never gained certification or use in his native France.

In both historical and scientific terms, the Global Sounding is such a beginning. It is a beginning that, rather than being buried for years in the customary bureaucracy of science and its funding—into which potentially disruptive measures such as this are usually dropped, often to be lost forever—*can immediately be put to use to meet increasingly urgent needs of our time.*

And so how are the questions of validity and reliability to be

MEASURING EVOLUTION

answered?

Here is my proposal. Being by now 81 with much else to do in whatever years are left me I will focus simply on providing a reliable base for publication and distribution initially through the Benjamin Franklin Press and its website (www.benjaminfranklinpress.com).

I invite—and indeed urge—all users of the Global Sounding to join in the following creative dialogue.

Send in brief reports of what happened: pros, cons, comments to benfranklin@benjaminfranklinpress.com.

These comments will be posted on the Franklin Press website for use in two ways: For the edification of prospective users. And as a source of raw data for use by younger generations to slog through the investment of all the money, time, and studies required to provide statistics for validation and reliability to everyone's satisfaction.

It could be said the Global Sounding as it stands today, through the background outlined in this guide to its use and in the end document "A Brief, Informal History of Measures of Global Well-being," already has a high degree of what is known as construct validity. But over time the rest of it should be pursued.

I offer this as a challenge to oncoming generations of idealistic young explorers, students as well as teachers, of the fascinating field of measurement.

Addendum from the Benjamin Franklin Press to users of the Global Sounding:

To help spread understanding and use of the Global Sounding as quickly and widely as possible worldwide, please send endorsements of the Global Sounding that we can publish for others to see.

DAVID LOYE

Send them to benfranklin@benjaminfranklinpress.com. Be sure to include your state, country of origin, and any important affiliations, e.g., positions, colleges, organizations. Please also include your email address and, if you wish, postal and fax addresses – all of which we will of course keep confidential, not publishing, with email addresses protected behind an electronic fortress of anti-spamming, anti-spy, and anti-virus software.

THE PROBLEM OF A SINGLE INDICATOR FOR CULTURAL EVOLUTION

A potentially controversial feature of the Global Sounding is its rigid adherence to a single pair of positive and negative statements for each prime indicator. This goes against the custom for most other indexes, for which answers for up to a dozen or more questions are cumulated to provide a rating or score for each prime indicator.

There are at least two reasons for this single indicator structure for the Global Sounding. One is that in building measures one always faces the question of a tradeoff between asking the large number of questions that measurement methodologists feel comfortable with and the requirement for ending up with something short enough and simple enough for use as well as comprehension by reasonably intelligent human beings. Out of my lifelong drive to unbottle progressive science and put it to the widest possible use the choice for the Global Sounding had to be weighted toward the latter concern.

The other reason is a bit more complex, as it involves some familiarity with the statistical methodology of factor analysis. From my years of using factor analysis to reduce usually a great variety of variables into a vastly shortened and simplified set of prime factors I became aware that this was actually one of the most powerful inborn tools of our own minds.

In other words, in trying to understand what is or can happen to us at every moment of our lives, we boil down a great range of possibilities into the most simple and forceful possible answer to guide our actions.

A striking example of the scientific use of this capacity and the power of the single indicator is the development of what are known as "unobtrusive measures," which I have often turned to in measures development. One decides on a single "unobtrusive" question or action designed to reveal a vital bit of information about another person or others without their being aware they are being tested. A classic unobtrusive measure of honesty, for example, is one drops a dollar bill on the ground, then hides behind a bush to see whether the person who picks it up keeps it or looks around and even goes in search of the rightful owner.

All things considered, I feel my use of single pair indicators for the Global Sounding is not only justified but will meet with gratitude by many users. In the case of an indicator for Cultural Evolution there do, however, remain problems.

The Special Case of Cultural Evolution

Use of single pair indicators for all the other levels and activities for the "tree of evolution" forced me to settle on a single pair of indicators for Cultural Evolution as a matter of satisfying the gestalt, or aesthetic or "clean line," appeal to users.

Here, however, I encountered the problem of the popular versus the scientific definition of cultural. To sociologists, anthropologists, and the evolution-minded scholarly community Cultural Evolution includes everything from above the level of psychological or personal evolution on the Global Sounding scale. That is, to begin to adequately measure it by this definition one would need to cumulate the Global Sounding "scores" for social, political, economic, educational, technological, moral, and spiritual evolution and the evolution of consciousness and expectations for action.

By contrast, the popular definition for the word "cultural" is a matter of association in the minds of most of us of symphonies, opera, art in all forms, great books, philosophy, as well as table manners, grammar and tone of speech, table manners, and whether one wears fashionable or unfashionable clothes.

Applying to the task at hand the rationale for boiling a great range of things into a single indicator, as explained above, I decided that "high priority for arts" for an indicator of progression and "low priority for arts" for an indicator of regression was a good choice, at least initially.

The conflict of the popular and scientific definition of what constitutes cultural evolution continued, however, to worry me until I came to see they were actually not in conflict. For what we usually see and deal with as separate entities are—as at last all the fields involved in evolutionary systems science make evident—generally linked to one another in certain over-riding systems. Thus, along with cultural evolution on all the levels and activities that the science involved in the Global Sounding defines, generally in tandem there is movement in the writing of music, literature, refinement of art, and all the rest of it.

All of it, for example, both by scientific and popular definition, is in a sense embraced within the over-riding system and concept of "civilization." To which, I would maintain, "high priority for arts" versus "low priority for arts" is as widely and deeply revealing an "obtrusive" indicator as one could hope to find.

On further consideration, I also feel the translation of this particular single pair indicator into Code 6 for the Global Sounding Moral Code extends this approach into the vital moral dimension so seldom tapped by prevailing measurement—and with the requisite bite of contemporary reality to make it more than another pious platitude.

"Culture," Code 6 states, "is *the most precious gift of evolution*, to be cherished and nurtured in the wonder of its diversity, rather than sliced and diced up for marketing to the rubes, or otherwise seized, shucked and twisted to serve low ends."

A BRIEF HISTORY OF
THE GENERAL EVOLUTION RESEARCH GROUP

This is an update of earlier brief histories published in *The Evolutionary Outrider* and *The Great Adventure and on the website for The Darwin Project (www.thedarwinproject.com).*

As with other all other groups, in the case of the General Evolution Research Group there are two histories: one sparse and formal, the other rich, engaging, and informal.

Formally, the General Evolution Research Group was formed in La Jolla, California, in 1986. Its purpose was to bring together a small group of scholars from a variety of disciplines and nations to explore possibilities for the development of a *general* (as differentiated from solely biological or paleontological) evolution theory. Following its formation, it has held meetings in Florence, Bologna, and Sardinia in Italy, Budapest in Hungary, Vienna in Austria, Turku in Finland, Potsdam in Germany, Toronto in Canada, and Carmel in the U.S. Its primary founder and leader was and is systems philosopher and general evolution theorist Ervin Laszlo. Its journal is *World Futures: The Journal of General Evolution*, with Laszlo as Editor and the original cofounding members of the General Evolution Research Group forming the Editorial Board. Currently, in addition to its independent existence, the General Evolution Research Group serves as a consultant scientific research body within the structure of Laszlo's formation of the international Club of Budapest.

Behind this sparse account, however, lies the other history, of the aspirations and frustrations of an unusual group of scholars at a dramatic turning point in the history of science and our species. In the account that follows can also be seen at work the dynamics of the very mix of evolution and chaos theory the Group was formed to explore. That is, in how its members met and tenuously, sporadically, but at times in meaningful ways came to work together, can be seen the interplay of the strange attractor, the basins, hypercyles, and most importantly, out of the bifurcations of the late 20th century, glimpses now and then of some vital movement toward the possibilities of the better world and better future.

A Pivotal Mission and the Early Days

The idea for what eventually became the Group began to form some years before 1986 in Ervin Laszlo's mind. Here had arrived this heady time in human history when, on one hand, there loom before us the escalating problems of the *world problematique*, which pose the question of whether our species is to fulfill or end itself. On the other hand, out of science had erupted the explosion of the new theories of nonlinear dynamics, of cybernetics, complexity, dissipative structures, self-organizing processes, all becoming popularly clustered within the general idea of "chaos theory." At the same time the old paradigm for evolution theory had been breaking down under the pressure of the intellectual and social logic for a *general* systems theory—that is, theory asserting the necessity of finding concepts in common across the disciplinary boundaries that too often have stifled creativity within science as well as science's ability to serve society.

What if one could be used to solve the other? That is, what if out of this double-edged explosion within science there might be found a way to apply this new mix of evolutionary theory and "chaos theory" to solutions for the personal, social, and cultural chaos of our time?

This was the idea—as expressed in various books, talks and papers—that originally captivated Laszlo, as a pioneering organizer for what was bit by bit becoming the new field of general evolution theory. Increasingly, it was also to captivate the handful of scholars that Laszlo began to draw together from many scientific disciplines and countries in attempts to move the idea forward.

As is usual for all ventures, a first attempt in this direction seemingly came to nothing. During the final years of the Cold War, scientists from both sides sought to transcend politics in a rapprochement to try to solve the mounting problems facing humanity. Out of this thrust had been formed an international organization with an equal representation of Western and Soviet bloc scholars, the International Institute of Applied Systems Analysis (IIASA) near Vienna. The Director General showed interest in Laszlo's idea. Hurriedly, he invited a handful of scholars from various countries in Europe and the U.S. with the requisite activist as well as scientific orientations to meet in Budapest to put together a proposal.

Particularly dramatic in retrospect was the "caravan" in which we set out from Budapest to drive to IIASA headquarters at the sumptuous Hapsburg hunting palace at Laxenburg, south of Vienna. Still up was the double row of barbed wire forming the barrier separating East from

West, along with scowling guards armed with machine guns, with scowling dogs tugging at the leash, and a grim checking of credentials and passes at each checkpoint for the crossing.

The IIASA project came to naught, but out of it came the mutual admiration, the friendships, and the preliminary working associations that laid the groundwork for what not too long afterward became the General Evolution Research Group. Involved in this critical formative stage, later to join Laszlo in becoming co-founding members of GERG, were biologist Vilmos Csanyi and computer scientist Georgy Kampis from Budapest; management theorist and futurist Penntti Malaska (with later Mika Pantzar also joining) from Finland; and from the U.S., Harvard astrophysicist Eric Chaisson (later to star in the development of the Hubble telescope), psychologist Jonathan Schull, historian Robert Artigiani, cultural evolution theorist Riane Eisler, and myself, a social psychologist and systems theorist.

The Formation of GERG, or a Bit of Order Out of Chaos

There also came out of this early attempt a flurry of ongoing contacts steadily advancing the idea. Pivotal in this regard was the meeting between Laszlo, Ilya Prigogine, and Jonas Salk at the "Discoveries 1985" Symposium in October of 1985 in Brussels. Of theorists whose work was most rapidly advancing the formation of a new theory of general evolution, Prigogine was by then the most influential— having received a Nobel Prize for his dissipative structures theory. Salk was of special interest in relation to the activist thrust for the developing project, having attained both world stature and enormous wealth for applying science to the needs of humanity in the case of the

MEASURING EVOLUTION

Salk vaccine. Both resonated powerfully to the idea, offering aid in any way possible.

A meeting in Santa Cruz, California, involving Laszlo, Eisler, and myself further enlisted the enthusiasm of the jovial eminent mathematician and chaos theorist Ralph Abraham. Then came the invitation from Jonas Salk that led to the Group's formal launching. His offer to provide funds for transportation and housing made it possible to at last draw together from the various parts of Europe and the U.S. what had now become the core group, i.e., from the original Budapesters Laszlo, Csanyi, Chaisson, Schull, Artigiani, Eisler and myself, with the addition now of Abraham and biologist John Corliss, an American then living in Budapest.

Again the project itself came to naught—in a most peculiar and even infuriating way I will some day write of elsewhere the hope had been that Salk and/or the Salk Institute might provide the housing and funding that by now seemed a bedrock necessity for any further movement of the idea forward. But in the aftermath of this disappointment, meeting in the hotel in La Jolla, California, where we were housed, there erupted the increasingly joyful and devil-may-care brain storming session out of which GERG came into being.

Based on my observation of the success of the "mom and pop think tanks" then erupting among futurists and other independent scholars, I pointed out there was nothing that said we couldn't go ahead on our own without funding, without a prestigous institutional attachment, without housing or tenure or infrastructure or all the other formal trappings that were now more often stifling than liberating scientific creativity throughout the world. There was really no good reason why we couldn't simply form our own group to go ahead and do what we wanted to do.

Names were bandied about, out of which "The General Evolution Research Group" emerged. Someone, however, soon remarked this would give us the acronym of GERG—which at first seemed horrible.

"Sounds like regurgitate," someone said. "Or gurgle," someone else said. "See the gurgling GERGian gargle," someone said. As our laughter became hysterical, with hair and beard like a great glowing white penumbra surrounding his ruddy face, Ralph Abraham struck a pose. "Today so-and-so the eminent GERGite received the Nobel Prize!" he offered.

So GERG it became. But soon the merriment died as all that we were up against once again sank in. We could get nowhere without our own journal in which to publish—for although I had no understanding of this at the time the old hands among us were aware of the grim fact that the present journals were all committed to constituencies wedded in one way or another to the past, and anything new in science must, as elsewhere, fight for years to wedge its way into established readerships.

It did now seem a hopeless undertaking. "But we already have it," Laszlo suddenly announced. He darted from the room with no further explanation, then soon returned beaming gaily. He explained he had called the publishers in London of a journal of which he was the Editor, *World Futures*. And Gordon and Breach had blessed going ahead with what now—as of that moment—became *World Futures: The Journal of General Evolution*, with all of us to serve as the new Editorial Board.

Some Developmental High Points

Thereafter the gorgeous GERGians, or GERGites, as it were, met whenever Laszlo persuaded a sponsor for a prestigious event to invest

MEASURING EVOLUTION

in us—which in itself was an important accomplishment historically. Contrary to the usual pattern of being unable to move without secure foundation funding or a settled institutional base, driven by his determination to see the purpose of GERG succeed—calling, I have always felt, on his early experience as a concert pianist—Laszlo now became one of the most skillful and influential "cultural impresarios " of his time.

An early highpoint was the meeting in Florence, Italy. In keeping with the difference between the U.S. and Europe that became so striking to me as I became exposed to more and more of Europe as a GERGite, each year instead of the "Car Capital" or "Football Capital," as it would have been for us, a new "Cultural Capital of Europe" was selected. Florence was it for 1986.

To provide a suitably important cultural event to commemorate the occasion, Laszlo sold the Florence powers-that-be on us, with naturally travel, housing, and all other expenses to be paid. With Italian philosopher (and subsequent GERG member) Mauro Ceruti, Laszlo organized a week-long symposium on the theme Abitare La Terra ("to live on Earth," with papers later to be sumptuously published in both English and Italian by the noted Italian publisher Feltrinelli). Key events included not only the maiden voyage presentations for our motley crew of GERGians, but also segments for presentations by eminent members of the Club of Rome, then riding high in the eye of the educated world, as well as the United Nations University.

Another high point replete with sumptuous program and attendant festooned literature was the selection of GERG to provide a symposium for the central cultural event commemorating the 900th Anniversary of the world's oldest university, the University of Bologna in Bologna,

Italy. A third high point was the first conference organized within the framework of the organization destined to become the only thing remotely like a "home" for us, the International Society for the Systems Sciences (ISSS). This was the gathering of the GEORGIAN clan organized by Vilmos Csanyi and Gyorgy Kampis (known more familiarly as "Villy" and "George") in 1987 in Budapest—which in retrospect emerges as a key original spiritual site for what later became GERG as well as the actual headquarters for Laszlo's later formation of the Club of Budapest.

Throughout this period GERG expanded somewhat. Into the official membership via Laszlo's personal contacts and selection came pioneering chaos theorist Ilya Prigogine from Belgium; the pioneering autopoesis theorist, Francisco Varela, from Chile and France; historian Ignazio Masulli and philosophers Mauro Ceruti and Gianluca Bocchi from Italy; mathematical biologist Peter Saunders and thermodynamicist Peter Allen from England; philosopher and systems theorist Min Jiayin from China; ecologist and philosopher Eduard Makarjan from Armenia in the Soviet Union; physicist Rudolf Treumann from Germany; management theorist Thomas Bernold from Switzerland; and from the United States, brain scientist Karl Pribram, evolutionary systems theorist Bela H. Banathy, psychologist Allan Combs, and systems scientist Alfonso Montuori, our journal's present Associate Editor.

More recently to the membership were added : :biologist and evolution theorist Stanley Salthe, futurist and evolutionary theorist Duane Elgin, and economist John Hisnanick of the U.S., and physicist Jurgen Kurths of Germany. During the Toronto gathering in connection with the World Congress of the Systems Sciences sponsored by ISSS, out of which this book emerged, sociologist Ray Bradley, systems scientist Ken Bausch, and evolutionary activists Alexander and Kathia Laszlo were added. Then prior to the 2003 ISSS/GERG meeting in Crete—to further the alliance between humanistic, transpersonal, and positive psychologists and evolutionary systems scientists proposed to help "kick start" the development of the "full spectrum, action-oriented" or fully human theory, as proposed in the Introduction to this book—the group was joined by psychologists Mihaly Csikszentmihalyi, leader in the development of positive psychology, and Stanley Krippner, past president of the Association for Humanistic Psychologist, and systems scientist Alexander Christakis, incoming president of the International Society for Systems Sciences and computer scientist and past ISSS president Bela A..Banathy..

Of particular importance in view of the often overwhelming tendency of 20th century international scientific groups to be exclusively male was the Group's increasing female membership. Historically, our fellow co-founder Riane Eisler became the first women to be included in the core working membership of a group devoted to evolutionary research as well as the first to contribute an influential new theory of cultural evolution. Over these years internationally renowned biophysicist Mae-Wan Ho from Great Britain, psychologist Singa Sandelin Benko from Sweden, political scientist Miriam Campanella, interdisciplinary educator Gerlind Rurik from Germany, social psychologist Maria Sagi, for a long stretch the Journal's Managing Editor, from Budapest, and evolutionary theorist Sally Goerner, and information theorist Susantha Goonatillake from Sri Lanka and now the U.S., were also invited by Laszlo to join the Group.

DAVID LOYE

The Way We Were and IT Was and Is:
A Glimpse at the Dynamics of the Paradigm
of PseudoDarwinian Mind

To those of us who originally aspired to see our world transformed by this venture, it must be admitted that GERG—as well as everything else one can think of—fell way short of the mark. At times, because of the difficulties of the old paradigm for science out of which we all came, it seemed we gathered together from around the world only to read papers born of separate disciplines, in separate scientific languages, with few of us really understanding what the "guy up there at the podium" was saying, immersed only in what we personally were going to say and glancing about the gathering to try to guess who might possibly pay any attention to our particular pearls of wisdom—and value them afterward. But informally, behind scenes, in the chats over breakfast, luncheons, arm in arm "out on the town" and during and after dinners, and then afterwards via e-mail and other communications internationally, there flowed between a handful of us Gergians the creative excitement and the sense of community and camaraderie that historically has been there at the making of all attempts at human advancement.

As professionally a student of as well as in some regards a purported authority on creativity, at times I used to try to get hold of what was different and hopeful and promising about us. To me the most memorable single finding was the degree to which most of us had come to scholarship not via the customary route of intimation piled upon intimidation that characterizes the traditional training for scientists. By this I mean the fact that the student valued by the conventional-minded academic has gone from high school into college into graduate studies

MEASURING EVOLUTION

with no dangerous interruptions that might taint his or her suitability for science. But I will never forget one session where a handful of us, suitably liquored and loose mouthed, confessed to the strange array of backgrounds out of which most of us had come.

There was, of course, Laszlo the ex-concert pianist to begin with. Villy Csanyi, it turned out, had originally been a writer for the Hungarian version of *Popular Mechanics*, or some such, as I recall. Riane Eisler had been a housewife, who getting fed up with washing dishes went back to school and became a lawyer, and then getting fed up with law became a self-educated systems scientist. And so it went on down the line to me and my confession I had originally been a newsman on a television station, a magazine editor, and a failed novelist in Oklahoma back in the Ed Murrow days.

The more I learned of science the more I found this story again and again in the case of the great contributors to their fields, as well as the fact that often their breakthroughs came while working, as we were, as independent scholars, most of us unattached either to universities or formal research institutions. Einstein the postal clerk. Darwin the mainly self-educated medical school and divinity studies dropout. The great formative sociologist Robert Park who earlier was a PR man for Booker T. Washington. The even greater sociologist Pitirim Sorokin who had been a secretary to Kerensky and later a general during the Russian revolution.

But then I began to see what has increasingly haunted and infuriated me about all of us—as well as about everybody else like us around the world working toward the same general goal. Here was this exceptionally bright, rather wondrously gifted group of people, pulled together to work for a truly noble and urgent purpose for society as well as science. And so we wrote our papers, and our books, and beyond occasionally meeting and reading our papers to one another we and others like us published—as I will come to—a truly astounding amount of original work bearing on the advancement of our species' understanding of who we are and where we can and should be headed, that is, of evolution and of evolution theory. And practically, functionally, as far as it having any appreciable impact in or on our world, we might just as well, as with the proverbial shipwrecked sailor on a desert island, have put it all in bottles and tossed them into the ocean in hope of a reader somewhere, some day.

It was out of this increasing sense of outrage and mounting concern that out of GERG I first founded The Darwin Project (www.thedarwinproject.com) and then The Benjamin Franklin Press (www.benjaminfranklinpress.com).

The problem was two-faced. One face was the fact of the vast cultural lag between science and society in the case of both professional publications and the news media. Almost all of our papers and books were disappearing into journals and academic publishers that reached at best the tiniest of fractions for readership, almost none of which had either the power or the interest in doing anything to try to better our world in any fundamental way. As for the news media, the tiny fraction of space open to anything dealing with evolution was almost entirely sopped up by stories either about Creationists battling to end the teaching of evolution, or the latest twist to the sociobiology of the "selfish gene," or the evolutionary psychology of experimental atop mathematical atop Tit for Tat game theory atop blind cave rat proof of still more and more selfishness rampant within human motivation at all levels including so-called altruism.

Gradually I came to see this other face to the problem that I write

MEASURING EVOLUTION

of in what became my Darwin Cycle for The Benjamin Franklin Press (i.e., *Bankrolling Evolution, Darwin on Love, Darwin's Lost Theory, The Derailing of Species,* and *Telling the New Story).* The challenge was to expose the scientific half-truth and the socially, politically, economically, and morally disastrous impact of the entrenched paradigm of PseudoDarwinian Mind.

While all of our output bobbed in bottles in parts of the ocean of consciousness way off the shipping lanes *this* was the prevailing story for almost all the books that were getting published and television specials that were getting made. It was a veritable flood of so-called science not only legitimizing the late 20th century wave of conservatism and proto-fascism re-possessing the U.S. and elsewhere but also the "no holds barred" rise of predatory new multinational power elites in the media and in business and government more generally.

Again and again the so-called science for all this was being contradicted not only by the work of groups such as ours but by hundreds of other scientists of whom I was becoming aware—almost all of it similarly messages in bottles bobbing in the waves far, far away from what was left of the mind of modern "man."

I also came to realize that I was one of few people in the whole of science at that time empowered to see this situation in anything approaching its true scope and depth. This is not meant as a foolish personal boast, but to point up the key factor here of a peculiarly offbeat background: in news and publications more generally originally; then training as a sociologist and systems scientist as well as a psychologist; then my experience over the better part of a decade as the research director of a large project fundamentally probing the impact of the media on us from an evolutionary perspective; and finally, most powerfully, my happenstance GERG involvement, which intimately involved me in the development of the new field of evolutionary systems science.

On discovering the extent to which Darwin has been used for over 100 years as the chief scientific legitimizer and false icon for all of this, I went to work relentlessly to try to change this situation on the behalf of GERG, and everything we had set out to do, but much, much more so on the behalf of all of us.

To this end I brought together the remnant GERGites for sessions during the World Congress for the Systems Sciences in Toronto in 2000, out of which came a special issue for our journal *World Futures* and publication of the book written by eleven of us to put the GERG work of over a decade to the challenge indicated by the title *The Great Adventure: Toward a Fully Human Theory of Evolution* (SUNY Press, 2004).

As indicate earlier, to this end I also formed The Darwin Project and The Benjamin Franklin Press.

The GERG Impact in Spite of It All

Throughout the history of the General Evolution Research Group its journal has served to hold it together by providing one of the most essential things for scientific advancement—a forum where the more independent and creative-minded who resonate to the creation of a more adequate theory of evolution and a science more adequate to the task of the advancement of our species can meet across national and disciplinary boundaries and freely exchange new ideas.

Originally published by Gordon & Breach, it was managed out of G&B offices in Newark, New Jersey, with editing and production in

MEASURING EVOLUTION

Madras, India, and distribution out of Brussels, Belgium. In 2001 another academic publisher Taylor & Francis bought out G&B and took over publication under the prestigious Routledge imprint.

(To subscribe and for further information about *World Futures*, go to the website for The Darwin Project, www.thedarwinproject.com, or Taylor & Francis, www.taylor&francis.com).

However dull or obscure our venturing might be at times, some idea of the range of mind for *World Futures: The Journal of General Evolution* can be gathered from the titles for a few special issues. *Evolutionary Consciousness*, edited by Bela H.Banathy (Vol.38:2-4). *Theoretical Achievements and Practical Applications of General Evolutionary Theory*, edited by Vilmos Csanyi (Vol.38:1-3). *The Presence of the Future: Values, Aptitudes and Behaviors for Life in the 21st Century*, edited by Francoise Parisot-Baratier (Vol.41:1-3). *The Path Toward Global Survival: A Social and Economic Study of 162 Countries*, edited by Hans-Wolff Graf (Vol.43:1-4). *The Quantum of Evolution*, edited by Francis Heyligen, Cliff Joslyn and Valentin Turchin (Vo.45:1-4). *Unity and Diversity in Contemporary Systems Thinking: Systemic Pictures at an Exhibition*, edited by J.D.R.de Radt and S.Strijbos (Vol.47:1). *The Concept of Collective Consciousness*, edited by Ervin Laszlo (Vol.48:1-4). *The Third Venture: Toward a Humanistic Theory of Evolution*, edited by myself (Vol.58:2-3), out of which came our SUNY Press book *The Great Adventure*.

Additionally, there are the many vital books of the General Evolution Research Group series originally published by Gordon and

Breach, most of which have been republished either by Taylor & Francis or its famous imprint Routledge. Most representative is the keynote volume: *The New Evolutionary Paradigm*, 1991, edited by Ervin Laszlo with foreword by Ilya Prigogine. Bringing together for the first time papers by our original core group articulating the purpose and horizon for the then new field of general evolution theory, this fresh and hopeful venture, if anything, surely was an historical contribution that deserves a better fate than now awaits it in the limbo in which most of what once was GERG now floats.

Unusual contributions were made by: Volume 1: *Nature and History: The Evolutionary Approach for Social Scientists*, by Ignazio Masuli. Volume 3: *The Age of Bifurcation: Understanding the Changing World*, by Ervin Laszlo. Volume 4: *Cooperation: Beyond the Age of Competition*, edited by Allan Combs. Volume 5: *The Evolution of Cognitive Maps: New Paradigms for the 21st Century*, edited by Ervin Laszlo and Ignazio Masulli, with Robert Artigiani and Vilmos Csanyi. Volume 6: *The Evolving Mind*, by Ben Goertzel. Volume 7: *Chaos and the Evolving Ecological Universe*, by Sally Goerner. Volume 8: *Constraints and Possibilities: The Evolution of Knowledge and the Knowledge of Evolution*, by Mauro Ceruti. *Merged Evolution* by Susantha Goonatilake. *Science, Education, and Future Generations* edited by Eric Chaisson and Tae Change Kim. *The Mind of Society* by Yvon Provencal. *The Great Transition* by Crawford Robb.

Still in print with other publishers, I believe, but in comparison with the thundering herd for the modern classics of selfishness and survival of the fittest for sociobiology and evolutionary psychology are bottles such as these similarly floating in limbo of the academic sea.

The Evolutionary Outrider: The Impact of the Human Agent on

MEASURING EVOLUTION

Evolution, an earlier book I edited honoring Laszlo with contributions by Fritjof Capra, Hazel Henderson, Karl Pribram, Riane Eisler, Ralph Abraham, Mae-Wan Ho, Ray Bradley, Maria Sagi, Paul Ray, Alfonso Montuori, Mauro Ceruti and Telmo Piavane (Praeger, 1998). *Changing Visions: Cognitive Maps Past, Present, and Future*, built out of one of our symposia by Ervin Laszlo, Robert Artigiani, Allan Combs, and Vilmos Csanyi (Praeger, 1996).

All in all, however bottled up—and all this is merely a fraction of the pages generated by the lodestone of GERG and its journal—this remains a repository of thinking about evolution unique within the 20th century, to which the 21st could do worse than return at some point to mine.

Should this happen, the miners will also find all the books we wrote that from time to time did manage to worm their way into mainstream publishing, most of which are still available as of this writing. Written independent of, but many of them I believe bolstered psychologically by our association within, GERG were books such as Laszlo's *The Whispering Pond*—a *Choice* selection for one of the outstanding scholarly books of 1997—as well as *Macroshift* more recently. Prigogine and Stenger's *Order and Chaos* and *The End of Certainty*. Eisler's international best-seller *The Chalice and the Blade* and *Sacred Pleasure, Tomorrow's Children, The Power of Partnership*. Pribram's *Brain and Perception*. Salthe's *Development in Evolution*. Csanyi's *Evolutionary Systems and Society*. The late Francisco Varela's (with Humberto Maturana) *Tree of Knowledge*. Chaisson's *Cosmic Dawn, The Life Era*, and *Cosmic Evolution*. Combs' award-winning *The Radiance of Being*. Montuori's *From Power to Partnership*. Abraham's *Chaos, Gaia, and Eros*. Ho and Saunders' *Beyond Neo-Darwinism*. And

DAVID LOYE

Elgin's *Awakening Earth* and *Promise Ahead.*

I should also hope those future probers of the prospect for a better world find the books of my Darwin Cycle as well as other books of mine had the impact in the end that I set out to give them (see book list for the Benjamin Franklin Press, www.benjaminfranklinpress.com)..

All in all, not so bad a showing for something that began with an episode like something out of a Cold War spy movie in Budapest in 1984, and then more formally out of despair and then our wild and willful laughter over an outrageous acronym in a hotel room in La Jolla in 1986.

THE TORONTO MANIFESTO

Within the past century two major ventures advanced the building of a scientific theory of evolution. The first was the building of the neoDarwinian paradigm during the early part of the century. The second was the sociobiological paradigm late in the century.

Both made important contributions to science, but at the same time both shared the same monumental blind side. Claiming the Darwinian heritage exclusively for themselves, they rigorously excluded everything that both in Darwin earlier and throughout the 20th century in the whole of science—particularly among creative evolution theorists linked together by a meeting ground in systems science—sought to expand evolution theory to capture the heights as well as the depths of humanity and our species' potential.

We are meeting here in Toronto to give new focus to what by now is a huge body of work routinely excluded from what is taught worldwide in our schools, in books reaching a general as well as scientific readership, and reinforced by television and other media as the one and only mainstream theory of evolution. We meet for what we hope may become a decisive new step toward what, if our species is to attain its potential, must become the successful *third venture* in this sequence to advance the scientific theory of evolution.

We are meeting to move beyond a science overwhelmingly focused on the *foundation* for evolution and the past to a renewal of emphasis on and a new vision of the human *superstructure* and the future.

This is a matter of increasingly urgent importance because it bears on what is to happen to our species at what has become the most crucial juncture in our evolution. We are meeting at a time of crisis in evolution, and crisis in the development of evolution theory. We are meeting to move beyond the cosmic world and the microbiological world into the human world of a radical expansion of brain, mind, consciousness, and, level by level upward, the escalating questions that now press upon us of personal, cultural, social, political, economic, educational, and technological evolution. Above all, as Darwin in actuality insisted, to this list must be added moral evolution. And as it is high time for science to recognize this continuing concern for billions of our species on this planet, to this list must be added spiritual evolution.

We are further meeting to move beyond a science committed solely to the passive role of the so-called wholly objective observer to the active role of science as partisan on the behalf of and advocate of *humanity*.

In short, we are meeting to look at what a full spectrum, action-oriented theory of evolution should look like, and how to actually build it. We are meeting to move beyond talking about it not to discard what we already have. We meet to expand and update our theory and our story of evolution to live up to the over 100,000 year investment by the life force in our species, and to fulfill the rising vision over all that time of what we both can become and should become.

MEASURING EVOLUTION

—a statement of purpose for the panels and meeting of the General Evolution Research Group, Monday, July 17, and Wednesday, July 19, 2000, during the World Congress of Systems Sciences in Toronto.

THE DARWIN PROJECT
www.thedarwinproject.com

The initiating question for the website of The Darwin Project is this.

As each new member of our species arrives on this earth, what do you want them to learn and live by?

The old "Darwinian" theory and story of "survival of the fittest" and "the celebration of selfishness"—by now fixed in our minds like the programming for robots driving our species toward destruction?

Or the new Darwinian theory and story based on the fact that in *The Descent of Man* Darwin wrote only twice about survival of the fittest -- but 95 times about love and 92 times about moral sensitivity.

The mission of The Darwin Project is to speed the shift in our homes, schools, and the media from only teaching destructive "first-half" Darwinism to the inspiring liberation of Darwin's long lost completing half—along with all the fields of modern science that support and expand Darwin's original full vision to reveal caring, love, moral evolution, and education as the prime drivers for human evolution.

In support of this project the following Darwin Project Council has been formed of over fifty distinguished American, European, and Asian scientists, educators, and media activists.

MEASURING EVOLUTION

Marcus Anthony - our first new member from the oncoming younger generation, to whom we older ones look for continuity of worldwide hopes and goals.

Angeles Arrien - anthropologist, founder and president of the Angeles Arrien Foundation for Cross-Cultural Education and Research, author of *The Four Fold Way*.

Ralph Abraham - mathematician, leading chaos theorist, professor emeritus University of Santa Cruz, co-founding GERG member and author *Chaos, Gaia, and Eros*.

Bela H. Banathy - pioneering evolutionary systems design theorist, past president International Society for the Systems Sciences (deceased 2003).

Kenneth Bausch - evolutionary systems scientist, executive director Institute for 21st Century Agoras, GERG member and author of *The Emerging Consensus in Systems Theory*.

Richard J. Bird - British psychologist and chaos theorist, past president Society for Chaos Theory in Psychology and Life Sciences, author of *Chaos and Life: Complexity and Order in Evolution and Thought*.

Howard Bloom - evolutionary theorist and activist, founding board member Epic of Evolution Society, author of *The Global Brain: The Evolution of Mass Mind from the Big Bang to the 21st Century*.

DAVID LOYE

Raymond Bradley - sociologist, director Institute for Whole Social Science, GERG member and author *Charisma and Social Structure: A Study of Love and Power, Wholeness and Transformation.*

Alexander Christakis - systems scientist, Club of Rome co-founder, past president International Society for the Systems Sciences, GERG member and director CWA Limited.

Allan Combs - neuropsychologist, systems theorist, and consciousness researcher, GERG member, editor of *Cooperation: Beyond the Age of Competition* and author of *The Radiance of Being.*

Gerald Cory, Jr. - neuroscientist, director Center for Behavioral Ecology, author of *The Reciprocal Modular Brain in Economics and Politics* and *Toward Consilience.*

Milhaly Csikszentmihalyi -psychologist and leading creativity theorist, director Quality of Life Research Center, Claremont Graduate University, GERG member and author of *The Evolving Self, Flow*, and *Creativity: Flow and the Psychology of Discovery and Invention.*

Riane Eisler - cultural historian and evolution theorist, developer of cultural transformation theory, co-founding GERG member, author of *The Chalice and the Blade, Sacred Pleasure, Tomorrow's Children*, and *The Power of Partnership.*

Duane Elgin - systems scientist, futurist, and media activist, GERG member, author of *Voluntary Simplicity, Awakening Earth, Global*

MEASURING EVOLUTION

Consciousness Change, and *Promise Ahead: Humanity's Journey Toward a Culture of Meaning.*

Sally Goerner - engineer, mathematician, and integral activist, co-founder and twice past president of The Society for Chaos Theory in Psychology and the Life Sciences, GERG member and author of *The Evolving Ecological Universe* and *After the Clockwork Universe.*

Rod Gorney - psychiatrist and media activist, adjunct faculty professor UCLA School of Medicine, founder and director Ashley Montagu Institute, author of *The Human Agenda: How to Be At Home in the Universe without Magic.*

Thom Hartmann - author and evolutionary and media activist, author of *The Prophet's Way, The Last Hours of Ancient Sunlight*, and *Unequal Protection: The Rise of Corporate Dominance and Theft of Human Rights.*

Hazel Henderson - futurist, economic theorist, evolutionary and media activist, developer of the Calvert-Henderson Quality of Life Indicators, author of *Building a Win-Win World, The Politics of the Solar Age*, and *Creating Alternative Futures.*

Mae-Wan Ho - British biophysicist and ethical activist, director Institute of Science in Society, GERG member and author of *Genetic Engineering, The Rainbow and the Worm*, and *Toward a New Ethics of Science, The Biology of Free Will.*

DAVID LOYE

Barbara Marx Hubbard - author and social innovator, president Foundation for Conscious Evolution, creator of EVOLVE and Gateway to Conscious Evolution, author of *Conscious Evolution* and *Emergence*.

Sohail Inayatullah - futurist and editor, professor Tamkang University in Taiwan, University of Sunshine Coast in Australia, and Queensland University of Technology; co-editor of the *Journal of Future Studies* and *New Renaissance*, co-editor of *Macrohistory and Macrohistorians*.

Min Jiayin - Chinese systems philosopher, research fellow Institute of Philosophy, Chinese Academy of Social Sciences, GERG member and author of *The Evolutionary Pluralism* and editor *The Chalice and the Blade in Chinese Culture*.

Jeffrey Kane - academic vice president of Long Island University, author of *Beyond Empiricism* and editor of *Education, Information, and Transformation: Essays on Learning and Thinking*.

Helena Knyazeva - Russian systems philosopher, evolutionary research scientist, Laboratory for Evolutionary Epistemology, The Russian Academy of Sciences, and author of *The Odyssey of Human Mind* and *Foundations of Synergetics*.

Stanley Krippner - psychologist, Saybrook Graduate School, former president Association for Humanistic Psychology, GERG member and author of *Human Possibilities*, co-author *Personal Mythology, Extraordinary Dreams*, and co-editor *Varieties of Anomalous Experience*.

MEASURING EVOLUTION

Hans Kung - internationally known German theologian, President of the Global Ethic Foundation of Tubingen University, author of *Does God Exist; Christianity and World Religion, Global Responsibility: In Search of a New World Ethic*, and editor, *Yes to a Global Ethic*.

Ervin Laszlo - systems philosopher and pioneering general evolution theorist, former research director United Nations, founder General Evolution Research Group (GERG), founder and president The Club of Budapest, author of *Evolution: The General Theory, The Choice: Oblivion or Evolution*, and over 30 other books on evolution and systems science.

Michael Lerner - Rabbi, psychologist, political theorist, editor Tikkun Magazine, chair The Tikkun Community, author of *The Politics of Meaning* and *The Left Hand of God: Taking Back Our Country from the Religious Right*.

Daniel Levine - mathematical psychologist and neural network theorist, former president International Neural Network Society, and author of *Introduction to Neural and Cognitive Modeling* and (forthcoming) *Common Sense and Common Nonsense*.

Bill Levis - treasurer, chief financial officer and board member, The Center for Partnership Studies, consultant to The Urban Institute and many social innovation start-ups, author of *Form 990 for Nonprofit Organizations*.

David Loye - psychologist, systems scientist and evolution theorist,

DAVID LOYE

former research director Program on Psychosocial Adaptation and the Future, UCLA School of Medicine, co-founding GERG member, author of *The Healing of a Nation, Bankrolling Evolution, Measuring Evolution*, and editor *The Great Adventure: Toward a Fully Human Theory of Evolution*.

Paul D. MacLean - widely considered one of the two greatest living brain scientists, former chief of the Laboratory of Brain Evolution and Behavior for the National Institute of Mental Health (NIMH), developer of the concept of the limbic system and the triune brain theory, author of *The Triune Brain in Evolution*.

Peter Meyer-Dohm - economist and leading German educator, chair International Partnership Initiative, chair, Academic Council, German Institute for Adult Education, German Society for Educational Sciences, German Institute for Distance Learning Research, German Institute for International Educational Research, and the Institute for the Pedagogy of Natural Sciences.

Ron Miller - historian and theorist of holistic and progressive education, founder of the Foundation for Educational Renewal and Paths of Learning and Encounter magazines, author of *What Are Schools For, Caring for New Life*, and *Free Schools, Free People*.

Alfonso Montuori - systems scientist, distance learning course pioneer, California Institute for Integral Studies, principal Evolutionary Strategies, associate editor World Futures, GERG member and author of *Evolutionary Competence* and *From Power to Partnership*.

MEASURING EVOLUTION

Nel Noddings - leading U.S. educator and moral theorist, Stanford University School of Education, author of *The Challenge to Care in Schools, Caring: A Feminine Approach to Ethics and Moral Education*, and *Starting at Home: Caring and Social Policy*.

Bruce Novak - educator, chair of the Assembly for Expanded Perspectives on Learning of the National Council of English Teachers (AEPL), chair of the Education Task Force of the Foundation for Ethics and Meaning.

John O'Manique - Canadian moral systems theorist, author of *The Origins of Justice: The Evolution of Morality, Human Rights and Law* (deceased 2003).

Barclay Palmer - educator, former head of Upper School Friend's Seminary, NYC; director Mirrors of Teaching, Teachers in Depth, board member Bowdoin Summer Music Festival.

Sister Ruthmary Powers - H.M., leading Catholic educator, Sisters of the Humility of Mary, Diocese of Pittsburgh, former superintendent, Catholic schools of Arizona, author *Partnership Education*.

Karl Pribram - widely considered one of the two greatest living brain scientists, former director Center for Brain Research at Radford University, developer of holographic and holonomic brain theory, GERG member and author of *The Language of the Brain, Brain and Perception*, and co-author of the classic *Plans and the Structure of*

DAVID LOYE

Behavior.

Raffi - composer, performer, recording artist, founder of The Child Honouring Institute, founder and president of Troubadour Music, author of *The Life of a Children's Troubadour* and Editor, *Child Honoring.*

Robert J. Richards - psychologist, historian, director Fishbein Center for the History of Science and Medicine, University of Chicago, author of *The Meaning of Evolution, The Romantic Conception of Life*, and the pivotal study for 20th century Darwinian research *Darwin and the Emergence of Evolutionary Theories of Mind and Behavior.*

Ruth Richards - psychiatrist and educational psychologist, Saybrook Graduate School, Harvard Medical School, and The McLean Hospital, co-developer of The Lifetime Creativity Scales, co-editor of *Eminent Creativity, Everyday Creativity, and Health.*

John Robbins - health revolutionary, author of *The Food Revolution, Diet for a New America*, and simultaneous global publication in many languages of *Healthy at 100.*

Nancy Roberts - professor Naval Postgraduate School, leader in movement to shift the emphasis from war to peace for the military, editor of *The Transforming Power of Dialogue* and author of *Transforming Public Policy.*

Frank Ryan - British physician, science theorist, author of *Darwin's Blind Spot: Evolution Beyond Natural Selection, The Eskimo Diet,*

MEASURING EVOLUTION

Tuberculosis, Virus X, and *Taking Care of Harry.*

Stanley Salthe - biologist and evolution theorist, GERG member and author of *Development and Evolution* championing a biology freed of the shackles of neoDarwinism and the integration of chaos, complexity, and other neglected theories into modern evolution theory.

David Scott - nuclear scientist, former chancellor University of Massachusetts, former provost Michigan State University, editor *Accountability and Control in Educational Settings.*

Tim Seldin - educator, president of the Montessori Foundation, chair of the International Montessori Council, author of *The Montessori Way, Building a World-Class Montessori School, Starting a New Montessori School, Celebrations of Life*, and *The World in the Palm of Her Hand.*

Christine Sleeter - leader in the field of multicultural studies, director Institute for Advanced Studies in Education, CSU Monterey Bay, author *Culture, Difference, and Power.*

Joseph Subbiondo - educator, president California Institute for Integral Studies, historian of linguistics specializing in the study of the relation between English words and the evolution of consciousness and a new language for science; editor, *John Wilkins and 17th Century British Linguistics.*

Brian Swimme - physicist and ethical cosmologist, director, Center for the Story of the Universe, California Institute for Integral Studies, author

DAVID LOYE

of *The Hidden Heart of the Cosmos, The Universe is a Green Dragon*, and *The Universe Story* (with Thomas Berry).

Michael Toms - co-founder of New Dimensions Radio and chief executive officer of the New Dimensions Broadcasting Network, board chairman emeritus of the California Institute of Integral Studies, author of *A Time for Choices, True Work, At the Leading Edge,* and *An Open Life.*

THE LOVELOCK STATEMENT OF GLOBAL URGENCY

The Earth is About to Catch a Morbid Fever That May Last as Long as 100,000 Years

by James Lovelock

© James Lovelock. First published in the wonderfully independent British newspaper *The Independent* January 16, 2006 *(www.independent.co.uk)*. Reproduced with permission.

Imagine a young policewoman delighted in the fulfilment of her vocation; then imagine her having to tell a family whose child had strayed that he had been found dead, murdered in a nearby wood. Or think of a young physician newly appointed who has to tell you that the biopsy revealed invasion by an aggressive metastasising tumour. Doctors and the police know that many accept the simple awful truth with dignity but others try in vain to deny it.

Whatever the response, the bringers of such bad news rarely become hardened to their task and some dread it. We have relieved judges of the awesome responsibility of passing the death sentence, but at least they had some comfort from its frequent moral justification. Physicians and the police have no escape from their duty.

This article is the most difficult I have written and for the same reasons. My Gaia theory sees the Earth behaving as if it were alive, and clearly anything alive can enjoy good health, or suffer disease. Gaia has made me a planetary physician and I take my profession seriously, and now I, too, have to bring bad news.

The climate centres around the world, which are the equivalent of the pathology lab of a hospital, have reported the Earth's physical condition, and the climate specialists see it as seriously ill, and soon to pass into a morbid fever that may last as long as 100,000 years. I have to tell you, as members of the Earth's family and an intimate part of it, that you and especially civilization are in grave danger.

Our planet has kept itself healthy and fit for life, just like an animal does, for most of the more than three billion years of its existence. It was ill luck that we started polluting at a time when the sun is too hot for comfort. We have given Gaia a fever and soon her condition will worsen to a state like a coma. She has been there before and recovered, but it took more than 100,000 years. We are responsible and will suffer the consequences: as the century progresses, the temperature will rise 8 degrees centigrade in temperate regions and 5 degrees in the tropics.

Much of the tropical land mass will become scrub and desert, and will no longer serve for regulation; this adds to the 40 percent of the Earth's surface we have depleted to feed ourselves.

Curiously, aerosol pollution of the northern hemisphere reduces global warming by reflecting sunlight back to space. This "global dimming" is transient and could disappear in a few days like the smoke that it is, leaving us fully exposed to the heat of the global greenhouse. We are in a fool's climate, accidentally kept cool by smoke, and before this century is over billions of us will die and the few breeding pairs of people that survive will be in the Arctic where the climate remains tolerable.

By failing to see that the Earth regulates its climate and composition, we have blundered into trying to do it ourselves, acting as if we were in charge. By doing this, we condemn ourselves to the worst form of slavery. If we chose to be the stewards of the Earth, then we are responsible for keeping the atmosphere, the ocean and the land surface right for life. A task we would soon find impossible - and something before we treated Gaia so badly, she had freely done for us.

To understand how impossible it is, think about how you would regulate your own temperature or the composition of your blood. Those with failing kidneys know the never-ending daily difficulty of adjusting water, salt and protein intake. The technological fix of dialysis helps, but is no replacement for living healthy kidneys.

My new book, *The Revenge of Gaia* (Penguin, 2006) expands these thoughts, but you still may ask why science took so long to recognize the true nature of the Earth. I think it is because Darwin's vision was so good and clear that it has taken until now to digest it. In his time, little was known about the chemistry of the atmosphere and oceans, and there would have been little reason for him to wonder if organisms changed their environment as well as adapting to it.

Had it been known then that life and the environment are closely coupled, Darwin would have seen that evolution involved not just the organisms, but the whole planetary surface. We might then have looked upon the Earth as if it were alive, and known that we cannot pollute the air or use the Earth's skin - its forest and ocean ecosystems - as a mere source of products to feed ourselves and furnish our homes. We would have felt instinctively that those ecosystems must be left untouched because they were part of the living Earth.

So what should we do? First, we have to keep in mind the awesome pace of change and realise how little time is left to act; and then each community and nation must find the best use of the resources they have to sustain civilization for as long as they can. Civilization is energy-intensive and we cannot turn it off without crashing, so we need the security of a powered descent. On these British Isles, we are used to thinking of all humanity and not just ourselves; environmental change is global, but we have to deal with the consequences here in the UK.

Unfortunately our nation is now so urbanized as to be like a large city and we have only a small acreage of agriculture and forestry. We are dependent on the trading world for sustenance; climate change will deny us regular supplies of food and fuel from overseas.

We could grow enough to feed ourselves on the diet of the Second World War, but the notion that there is land to spare to grow biofuels, or be the site of wind farms, is ludicrous. We will do our best to survive, but sadly I cannot see the United States or the emerging economies of China and India cutting back in time, and they are the main source of emissions. The worst will happen and survivors will have to adapt to a hell of a climate.

Perhaps the saddest thing is that Gaia will lose as much or more than we do. Not only will wildlife and whole ecosystems go extinct, but in human civilization the planet has a precious resource. We are not merely a disease; we are, through our intelligence and communication, the nervous system of the planet. Through us, Gaia has seen herself from space, and begins to know her place in the universe.

We should be the heart and mind of the Earth, not its malady. So let us be brave and cease thinking of human needs and rights alone, and see that we have harmed the living Earth and need to make our peace with

MEASURING EVOLUTION

Gaia. We must do it while we are still strong enough to negotiate, and not a broken rabble led by brutal war lords. Most of all, we should remember that we are a part of it, and it is indeed our home.

> James Lovelock is an independent environmental scientist and Fellow of the Royal Society. *The Revenge of Gaia* is published by Allan Lane Books, an imprint of Penguin Books, U.K., and by Basic Books in the U.S.

NOTES AND REFERENCES

1. The uncovering of Darwin's completion for his theory of evolution is reported in seven published and forthcoming books by David Loye. Editor, *The Great Adventure* (SUNY Press, 2004), with foreword by Mihaly Csikszentmihalyi and chapters by Ervin Laszlo, Stanley Salthe, Riane Eisler, Raymond Trevor Bradley, Aleco Christakis, Kenneth Bausch, Sally Goerner, Alfonso Montuori, Allan Combs, and Ruth Richards. Author, *Bankrolling Evolution, The Measuring Evolution, Darwin in Love, Darwin's Unfolding Revolution, The Derailing of Species,* and *Telling the New Story.* See The Darwin Anniversary and The Darwin Anniversary Book Cycle in closing documents for this book for brief descriptions. See the website for the Benjamin Franklin Press for further information and publication dates: www.benjaminfranklinpress.com.

2. See Ilya Prigogine and Isabelle Stengers, *Order Out of Chaos* (Bantam, 1984). (This is a rather unintelligible book through an attempt to popularize the subject. Far better is the classic work relating the core for most of this new work to evolution theory, Erich Jantsch's *The Self-Organizing Universe* (Pergamon Press, 1980).

3. See Edward Lorenz, "Irregularity: A Fundamental Property of the Atmosphere," *Tellus*, 1984, pp.98-110.

4. See Norbert Weiner, *Cybernetics* (MIT Press, 1948/1965).

5. See Loye, D., and Eisler, R. "Chaos and Transformation: The Implications of Natural Scientific Nonequilibrium Theory for Social Science and Society." *Behavioral Science* (1987): 32, 1, pp.53-65. Loye, D. Chaos and Transformation: Implications of Non-Equilibrium Theory for Social Science

and Society. In Laszlo, E., Ed., *The New Evolutionary Paradigm*. New York: Routledge, 1990.

6. For a good account of the significance of the life and works of Kant, Freud, Durkheim, Piaget, and many others in this regard, see D.Loye, (forthcoming) *The River and the Star: The Lost Story of the Great Explorers of the Better World.*

7. See D.Loye, Editor, *The Evolutionary Outrider: The Impact of the Human Agent on Evolution* (Praeger, 1998); D.Loye, Editor, *The Great Adventure: Toward a Fully Human Theory of Evolution* (SUNY Press, 2004).

8. This seemingly inconceivable fact, which can be glimpsed in the isolation and general lack of awareness of the kind of work of which the GERG venture is representative, is probed in detail in D.Loye (forthcoming)*The Derailing of Species.*

9. See John R. Graham, *MMPI-2: Assessing Personality and Psychotherapy.* (Oxford University Press, 1999).

10. For widely recorded, specific data on Bushist policies, see D.Loye, *Bankrolling Evolution: Money, Science, and Politics.*

11. See Wikipedia (www.en.wikipedia.org) for an excellent account of the development of the Stanford-Binet IQ test.

12. See, e.g., D.Loye, *An Arrow Through Chaos* (Park Street Press, 2000); Robin Robertson and Allan Combs, *Chaos Theory in Psychology and the Life Sciences* (Erlbaum, 1995); and Fred Abraham and Kenneth Gilgen, *Chaos Theory in Psychology* (Praeger, 1995).

13. Chapter Five: To calculate "composite results." For the group scores for each of the 15 indicators are added. Totals are then divided by the number of participants to obtain an average score for each indicator. These averaged totals are then added to obtain the total score for the group as a whole.

For example, let us say ten decision-makers are involved in deciding for or

MEASURING EVOLUTION

against a particular proposal. Their totals for each of the 15 indicators are divided by 10, to provide a "composite result" for each indicator. Then these 15 composite results are totaled to provide a composite total score.

Obviously, in many cases this will result in fractions other than the those we indicate in "round numbers" for ease of illustration.

14. See James Lovelock, *The Revenge of Gaia: Why the Earth Is Fighting Back - and How We Can Still Save Humanity* (Allen Lane, 2006); Lynn Margulis, *Symbiotic Planet: A New Look at Evolution* (Weidenfeld & Nicolson, 1998); and the excellent account of Gaia theory online in Wikipedia (www.en.wikipedia.org).

15. See Max Weber, *On the Methodology of the Social Sciences* (Free Press,1949); Gunnar Myrdal, *Value In Social Theory* (Harper, 1958); Abraham Maslow, *The Psychology of Science* (Harper,1966). See also Gideon Sjoberg and Roger Nett, *A Methodology for Social Research* (Harper, 1968); Eugene J. Webb, Donald T. Campbell, Richard D. Schwartz, and Lee Sechrest, *Unobtrusive Measures* (Sage, 1999).

16. See Hortense Powdermaker, *Stranger and Friend* (Norton, 1966).

17. See, e.g., Riane Eisler, *The Chalice and the Blade* (Harper, 1987); Duane Elgin, *Promise ahead: A vision of hope and action for humanity's future* (Morrow, 2000); Ervin Laszlo, *The Choice: Oblivion or Evolution* (Tarcher,1994); James Lovelock, *The Revenge of Gaia: Why the Earth Is Fighting Back - and How We Can Still Save Humanity* (Allen Lane, 2006); *World Scientists' Warning to Humanity* (Union of Concerned Scientists, 1993).

NOTE: See *Bankrolling Evolution: Money, Science, and Politics* for a comprehensive bibliography. A separate bibliography and index will be added to later editions of this book.

DARWIN ANNIVERSARY REPORT

February 12, 2009, will mark the 200th anniversary of the birth of Charles Darwin, long considered the world's greatest scientist for the bold statement and impact of his theory of evolution. The year will also honor the 150th anniversary of the publication of Darwin's *On the Origin of Species*.

Here's a report with URLs for more information about: The major traveling museum exhibit. New voyage of the full-size, sailing replica of the Beagle. Darwin Day Celebration. The "Great Adventure" Darwinians. Darwin Anniversary Book Cycle. The booming movement of progressive religious support for the science of evolution. And much more.

See www.darwinanniversary.com for regular updates for The Darwin Anniversary Report including immediate access to the websites for all events.

Darwin Anniversary Museum Tour

From November, 2005, through May, 2006, Americans got an eye- and mind-opening look at Darwin from A to Z in a major exhibition at the American Museum of Natural History in New York City.

The exhibit has moved on to Boston, Toronto and Chicago before going to the Natural History Museum in London to celebrate the 200th anniversary of Darwin's birth in 2009.

From a review in *The American Scientist:* "We see his [Darwin's] passion for the natural world, evidenced by his energetic beetle hunting as a child, transform into the collecting of crucial specimens on the voyage of the Beagle.

..This exhibit is intellectual history at its most thrilling, as we witness Darwin, with his deceptively simple new theory, make a whole set of predictions about the living world... His tentative early speculations yield to his increasing realization that evolution by natural selection accounts elegantly for observations in a range of disciplines. His anxiety about revealing his theory to the outside world ("It's like confessing a murder," he would write to his friend Joseph Hooker) fades as he resolves to bring all of the history of life—including the origin of Homo sapiens—under the umbrella of evolutionary thinking."

For more, go to: www.americanscientist.org/template/BookReviewTypeDetail/assetid/49582

The wellknown American scientist Niles Eldredge is gaining much credit for originating and putting the exhibit together as its curator. For a regular update on the tour and Darwinian doings, see Eldredge's rollicking and engaging blog: www.nileseldredge.com.

The New Voyage of the Beagle

Certainly the most colorful and impactful event underway will be the new voyage of the Beagle. This was the famous journey and the book the young Darwin wrote about his shipboard adventure around the world in his mid-twenties.

A full-size, seaworthy replica of the Beagle is being built in the seaport of Milford Haven in Pembrokeshire county in England. In 2009, a team of enterprising scientists will go aboard to re-enact the original cruise that took Darwin from England to South America, then to the famous Galapagos Island, to Tahiti, to Australia, and finally around the horn of Africa back up the coast to England again.

Other ships will follow the new Beagle with film crews for movies and television and reporters for all media for regular reports as—with the drama of sails, row on row upward, billowing out from its masts—the resurrected vessel moves from port to port around the world.

The Beagle Project Pembrokeshire was founded by David Lort-Phillips, descendent of a sailor and later commander of the Beagle back in Darwin's time, and Peter McGrath, author and yachtmaster.

For more information, see URL: www.thebeagleproject.com.

See www.aboutdarwin.com for a wonderfully animated map of the voyage on this remarkable website created by David Leff, who modestly claims to be only "an amateur scholar of the History of Science."

Darwin Anniversary Book Cycle

To complement and fill out the prevailing story and science, the Benjamin Franklin Press is publishing an unusual six book Darwin Anniversary Book Cycle to cover the startling findings and implications of a recently uncovered new side to Darwin's story and theory of evolution.

Counter to the widespread impression that selfishness and "survival of the fittest" is the primary drive for human and all other levels of evolution, this new series of six books explores the brain, social, and evolutionary systems science corroborating Darwin's own long ignored emphasis on moral sensitivity, love, and education as primary factors for evolution at the human level.

For more information see URL: www.benjaminfranklinpress.com.

The Darwin Day Celebration

Originated by Dr.Robert Stephens at Stanford University in 1995, and formalized by Stephens and Amanda Chesworth in 2000, in a rather short time the Darwin Day Celebration now has a sparkling and information-loaded website providing a visually appealing guide to Darwin's life, evolution theory, and news and views of doings in the world of Darwinana.

A particularly advanced feature is a year by year guide to relevant Darwin

Day events from 1994 projected through 2011. You can register your event with them. The site offers guidance—and in effect good free advertising—to people wanting to organize new events honoring Darwin during and following these Anniversary years.

It also has the rather amazing feature of a translation service of considerable importance for enlisting global enthusiasm for the Darwin Anniversar—with obvious implications for offsetting the anti-science, anti-evolution as well as anti-democracy drive by regressive authoritarian religious organizations and movements globally.

They offer computer translations into French, German, Italian, Portugese, and Spanish, with Korean and Japanese in an early stage. They're looking for human translators for Portugese, German, French, Italian, Russian, Korean, Chinese, Japanese, and other major languages.

URL: www.darwinday.org.

Great Adventure Darwinians

A growing movement of considerable scientific and social importance during these Darwin Anniversary years is of what might be termed, after a recent "flagship" book, the Great Adventure Darwinians.

Otherwise termed "the second Darwinian revolution," and "the third venture," the new movement is a social action-oriented association of thousands of scientists who, versus Creationists, present a common front with all other evolutionists in recognizing the modern originating importance of Darwin's theory and the scientific fact of evolution. But they differ from the prevailing understanding of evolution theory in important new ways. Scientifically emergent out of physics, advanced biology, systems science, chaos, complexity, cybernetic, and self-organizing theories, often also recognizing the place for spirituality in evolution, they are linked together in joint ventures aimed at expanding and updating evolution theory beyond prevailing earlier model theories.

MEASURING EVOLUTION

Conferences, new books, and other events will be reported online on the regularly updated Darwin Anniversary Report: www.darwinanniversary.com. For a "flagship" book, see *The Great Adventure: Toward a Fully Human Theory of Evolution* (SUNY Press, 2004) with an online "look inside" on www.thedarwinproject.com/adventure/book.html). For a brief statement of the "third venture" perspective, see the Toronto Manifesto: www.benjaminfranklinpress.com/manifesto.html.

For a look at international scientific and other organizations involved in this movement, see: International Society of Systems Sciences (ISSS): www.isss.org. The General Evolution Research Group (GERG): www.thedarwinproject.com/gerg/gerg.html. The Darwin Project: www.thedarwinproject.com. The Santa Fe Institute: www.santafe.edu. The Society for Chaos Theory in Psychology and the Life Sciences: www.societyforchaostheory.org. American Society for Cybernetics: www.asc-cybernetics.org. The Club of Budapest: www.clubofbudapest.org. The Institute for 21st Century Agoras: www.globalagoras.org. And The Club of Rome: www.clubofrome.org.

Humanist Darwin Days

A basic participant in the origination with Dr. Stephens of the Darwin Day Celebration, now annually sponsoring Darwin Days, is the Humanist Community. Their website focuses on items such as the origin and history of Darwin Day, an International Celebration of Science and Humanity, and Evolution vs. Creationism: The Anatomy of a Controversy, or Why People Have a Hard Time Accepting Darwin. Activities primarily in the San Francisco Bay area are listed at: www.humanists.org/dday.htm.

They also heartily recommend interested parties go to the website for ..

The Secular Student Alliance

DAVID LOYE

This is an exciting development for oldsters who feel we've done a very poor job of arousing our species to what's at stake for us and our planet in understanding Darwin and evolution theory, versus the rising tide of global indifference and ignorance.

The full title signals hope for the future: Secular Student Alliance: Mobilizing Students for a New Enlightenment. Physically located in the politically regressive state of Ohio, the Secular Student Alliance now has chapters in the following amazing list of college campuses. In: Bangladesh, Cameroon, Canada, Ghana, Iceland, Nigeria, Uganda, United Kingdom, and in the USA, Alabama, California [with 8 campuses], Colorado, Connecticut, Delaware, Florida, Georgia, Iowa, Idaho, Illinois, Kansas, Kentucky, Louisiana, Massachusetts, Michigan, Minnesota, Missouri, North Carolina, New Mexico, New York, Ohio [with 5 campuses], Oklahoma, Oregon, Pennsylvania, South Carolina, Tennessee, Texas [with 9 campuses], Virginia, and Wisconsin.

URLs: www.secularstudents.org and www.secularstudents.org/affiliates Contact: ssa@secularstudents.org.

The Clergy Letter Project

In the drive to end the senseless, time-wasting, and regressive "Creationists versus Evolutionists" battle, potentially very important in terms of long range impact is the new Clergy Letter Project.

Feeling that "for far too long, strident voices, in the name of Christianity, have been claiming that people must choose between religion and modern science," this Project was launched by Michael Zimmerman, Dean of the College of Liberal Arts and Sciences at Butler University in 2004.

A "Darwin Sunday" and an "Evolution Sunday" have been organized to encourage ministers "to discuss the compatibility of religion and science with their congregations through sermons and/or discussion groups." In 2006, 467 Congregations from every State in the U.S. and the District of Columbia participated. More than 10,000 Christian clergy have now signed The Clergy Letter asserting the compatibility of progressive religion with progressive science. Featured on their website are pro-Darwin sermons of members of The Clergy Letter Project.

URL: www.butler.edu/clergyproject/clergy_project.htm.

Evolution of Religion Conferences and Revivals

January 3-9, 2007, an International Conference on the Evolution of Religion will [or by now, did] further explore increasing interest in the interface between progressive science and religion at the Makaha Resort near Waianae, Oahu, in Hawai.

Though this event will be over within a relatively short time after this book is published and the Darwin Anniversary Report is launched online, we're recording it because of its significance as the outgrowth of an ongoing series of "Evolutionary Salons" launched by Michael Dowd and Connie Barlow.

Dowd has been called "North America's evolutionary evangelist." He and his wife, a popular science writer, live permanently on the road, teaching and preaching "the marriage of science and religion for personal and planetary wellbeing" in churches, schools, and living rooms across the continent. Under discussion is the idea of launching *progressive evolutionary science-oriented* old time, new message, evangelical style revivals. Some may shudder at the idea—but not politically-astute progressives concerned by the rapid spread of the power of rightwing anti-science religion in America.

As an indicator of globally mounting interest in a side to Darwin and the theory of evolution reaching out beyond both traditional science and traditional religion, the Dowd-Barlow website generates more than 250,000 hits per month.

URL: www.thegreatstory.org. URL for Hawaii conference and aftermath: www.evolutionofreligion.org.

DAVID LOYE

Shrewsbury Darwin Day Festival

Shrewsbury, England—with the support of Charles Darwin's great-great grandson, Randall Keynes, author of one of the best new books on Darwin—has a Darwin Day Festival.

Shrewsbury is where Charles Darwin was born. This small town in the Western Midlands near the Welsh border has had a week long Celebration in early February for the past four years. However, in 2005 they expanded the Celebration to a month-long affair. This impressive Celebration will feature films, speakers, and plays, together with "many activities for citizens and visitors alike."

URL: www.darwinshrewsbury.org.

Something to Think About

Abraham Lincoln, emancipator of the American slaves, and Charles Darwin, emancipator of the human mind, were both born on the same day: February 12th, 1809.

For a glimpse at his long ignored "Lincolnesque" completion for his theory of evolution, here is what Darwin specifically wrote in his book on *human* evolution, *The Descent of Man*:

> "Important as the struggle for existence has been and even still is, yet as far as the highest part of our nature is concerned there are other agencies more important. For the moral qualities are advanced either directly or indirectly much more through the effects of habit, by our reasoning powers, by instruction, by religion, etc., than through natural selection." (See Darwin's *summarizing conclusions* for *The Descent of Man*, page 404, Princeton Press Edition).
>
> And: "But the more important elements for us are love, and the distinct emotion of sympathy."

MEASURING EVOLUTION

And of how: "The birth both of the species and of the individual are equally parts of that grand sequence of events that our minds refuse to accept as the result of blind chance. The understanding revolts at such a conclusion."

THE DARWIN ANNIVERSARY BOOK CYCLE

This is a quick summary of the six new books on Darwin and evolution theory the Benjamin Franklin Press is publishing to honor the Darwin Anniversary. (See www.benjaminfranklinpress.com for unusual integrated covers for all six books and publication dates for availability via Amazon, Barnes & Noble, Powells and other online book sellers and via Ingrams for books stores).

Bankrolling Evolution. Using the new approach of evolutionary systems science foreshadowed by Darwin, the Darwin Anniversary cycle begins with this book. It brings to life the significance of Darwin's long-ignored morally- and action-oriented completion of his theory of evolution for meeting our current immense environmental and political challenges.

Measuring Evolution. This is a user's guide to the Global Sounding, a new measure of local, national, and global health and wellbeing based on a reconstruction of Darwin's completed theory and the findings of thousands of modern scientists that corroborate it. Designed to provide a guide to more effective action for bettering our world, this measure monitors the "new Darwinian" full range for evolution—from cosmic, chemical, and biological, to cultural, moral, and spiritual evolution.

Darwin's Lost Theory. This is the core book uncovering Darwin's revolutionary, yet strangely ignored, "second half" for his theory of evolution. It tells of how Darwin's observations of the primacy of mutual aid, education, love, and moral sensitivity for human evolution were "buried in plain sight" during 100 years of our social and scientific fixation on "survival of the

MEASURING EVOLUTION

fittest"—even though Darwin specifically insisted "other agencies" are more important at our level of evolution. It shows how recognition of this "lost" Darwinian theory could have changed the 20th century for the better—and can still help save the 21st.

Darwin on Love. Long scattered throughout Darwin's writings are ninety five stories of the love and sex life of an intriguing range of animals. Through the charm and delight of Darwin's own love story— and the insights and humor of these ninety five stories of love and sex for the first time brought together here—this book provides an engaging introduction to the new story and theory of Darwin for readers of all ages.

The Derailing of Evolution. Detailing the dramatic, century-long, battle of progressive scientists against the distortion of Darwin's theory, this book reveals the astonishing power of how our minds can be seized by an overriding paradigm that—with the best intentions of even the brightest of minds—can blindly drive us toward destruction. It underlines the importance of a new Darwinian model combining both parts of Darwin's original vision of what drives us ahead, checks us in place, or drives us backward in evolution.

Telling the New Story. The first of a series on a new updating and expansion for the science and story of evolution by innovative educators. From grade school through graduate studies—with crucial attention to the media—the series will provide teacher's guides and curricula designed to accelerate a shift in education from the fixation on old model Darwinism to a new science and story of "a place for every one of us in evolution."

PRE-PUBLICATION REVIEWS OF
DARWIN'S LOST THEORY
BY SCIENTISTS AND EDUCATORS

Because of the fresh and startling nature of the books of our Darwin Anniversary Book Cycle, these pre-publication reviews of the initiating book for this Cycle by internationally known scientists and educators offer essential information for an expanding global readership and interest in Darwin during these special Anniversary years.

The following experts are almost all members of one or more of four of the main international groups involved in advanced evolution research and theory: the General Evolution Research Group, the International Society for Systems Sciences, the Society for Chaos Theory in Psychology and the Life Sciences, and the Washington Evolution Studies Society.

If you are an authority on Darwin, evolution theory, social or natural science, scientific education, or social or environmental activism and wish to add your views to these endorsements, please send them to benfranklin@benjaminfranklinpress.com.

✺✺✺

"David Loye's rediscovery of the 'real' Darwin rehabilitates one of the most cited yet also most misunderstood scientists of all times: Darwin the visionary, the moral thinker, not the mechanistic random-evolutionist, as his

MEASURING EVOLUTION

followers have it. For this rediscovery not only biologists, and not only all natural and social scientists, but everyone concerned with our understanding of evolution on this planet owes Loye a deep debt of gratitude."

Ervin Laszlo, founder of the General Evolution Research Group and the Club of Budapest, Editor of *World Futures: The Journal of General Evolution*, former Director of Research for the United Nations Research and Development Program, author of *Evolution: The General Theory, The Interconnected Universe*, and over 30 other books on evolution and systems science.

※※※

"The idea that Charles Darwin himself believed that the final climb to human civilization required the enactment of a principle of moral conduct far above the "selfish gene" concept so prevalent in today's popular accounts comes as a surprise. But the fact that he argued at length and with passion for the recognition of this principle, along the way anticipating scientific concepts from far beyond his time, and further that this work has been utterly disregarded by the official keepers of evolutionary theory ever since, boggles the mind.

"Here, prominent social and evolutionary theorist David Loye treats us to a scientific mystery story of the first order. Taking us back to the final years of Darwin's life, in his home at Down and during the summer of 1868 at his Freshwater cottage on the Isle of Wight, where he struggled to find expression for the thoughts that would form the core of *The Descent of Man*, Loye leads us with sure steps through Darwin's emerging work, and through the Great Invisible Book that lies within, unfolding its vast implications and leaving no doubt that Darwin's long ignored plea for a larger vision of human nature is still relevant in the modern world and more desperately needed than ever.

"This is an immensely important book with an engaging and easy style that will recommend it to readers of all backgrounds and interests."

Allan Combs, psychologist and evolution theorist, author of *The Radiance*

DAVID LOYE

of Being, psychology department, formerly University of North Carolina in Asheville, now Saybrook Institute and the California Institute for Integral Studies in San Francisco.

※※※

"This is the most exciting, most revealing book on Darwin that I have ever read. More than any other, it has restored the full grandeur to Darwin's thesis as it evolved, as living beings evolved, from the survival of the fittest, through altruistic acts in social communities to the final affirmation of a desire for good, more compelling even, than our desire for self-preservation."

Mae Wan Ho, biophysicist and evolution theorist, author of *The Worm and the Rainbow*, *Genetic Engineering*, and editor, *Beyond Neo-Darwinism: The New Evolutionary Paradigm*, biology department, The Open University, London

※※※

"Once in a decade or more a special book comes along, of urgent importance to the intellectual discourse of the time: Darwin, Freud, Jantsch, Lovelock. David Loye's *Darwin's Lost Theory* is this special. It represents the culmination of the Chaos Revolution, and the critical application of General Evolution Theory. It corrects an oversight in the history of science which has swerved the modern world off its track. It provides the key to the reintegration of the sciences: physical, biological, and social. It can be the spark to jumpstart the social sciences to a new golden age of relevance to popular culture, by clearly showing how evolution theory bears on the survival of our species and our biosphere. In this work Loye has brought his unique erudition to an enormous and critical task, and carried it off with genius. We urgently need this book, and we need it now."

Ralph Abraham, mathematician and chaos theorist, author of *Chaos,*

MEASURING EVOLUTION

Gaia, and Eros: A Chaos Pioneer Uncovers the Three Great Streams of History, Dynamics: The Geometry of Behavior, and *The WEB Empowerment Book*, Professor Emeritus, University of California at Santa Cruz.

※※※

"One of the central difficulties in modern biology is how to account for the origin of those human features we are inclined to consider superior, traits such as morality, ethics, rationality, self-consciousness, and spiritual experiences. The difficulty is that they must have arisen in evolution from a manner of living that did not contain them. *Darwin's Lost Theory* shows that Darwin saw this, and that his vision of a detailed answer to the question in terms of human emotional and cognitive development beyond the basic operation of natural selection has not been acknowledged. It is important that this part of Darwin's writing be recovered, as Loye does very clearly and in a compelling manner in this book. *Darwin's Lost Theory* also provides important insights into the cognitive processes of Darwin himself and the history of biological thinking."

Humberto R. Maturana, professor, Department of Biology, The University of Chile, developer of the concept and theory of autopoiesis, author (with Francisco Varela) of *Autopoiesis and Cognition* and *The Tree of Knowledge*, and (with G. Verden-Zoller) of *Amore e Gioco* and other books in Italian, German, and Spanish.

※※※

"In his book on Darwin's 'lost theory,' Loye grips the reader's imagination somewhat as if glued to watching him put together a giant jig-saw puzzle showing the whole sweep of evolution in the light of both former and recent thinking. I have been particularly fascinated by Loye's discovery of the connection between Darwin's projection of the evolutionary development of the moral sense and my own brain research. In the notebook of 1838 Darwin asked himself, 'May not moral sense arise from . . . our strong sexual, parental, and social instincts?' This is point for point what I found 100 years later in my own extensive exploration of the primate brain in regard to primal sex-related functions. I had summed up these findings by saying that 'in the complex organization of the evolutionarily old and new structures under consideration, we presumably have a neural ladder, a visionary ladder, for ascending from the most primitive sexual feeling to the highest level of altruistic sentiments.' I am very impressed with how Loye shows that Darwin expanded this core insight into the full theory so long overlooked in *The Descent of Man."*

Paul D.MacLean, M.D., Senior Research Scientist, National Institute of Mental Health, evolutionary brain theorist, author of *The Triune Brain in Evolution.*

※※※

"At the end of ten years studying the application of chaos and other new theories to human evolution and researching the moral studies of the founding fathers of social science, David Loye unearthed a major scientific treasure: Darwin's 'hidden' theory of moral choice. Carefully piecing together fragments scattered in *The Descent of Man* and in Darwin's other writings, Loye reconstructs the 'hidden' theory and shows that Darwin believed that love, rather than the "selfish gene", is the prime mover in human evolution. Loye's book offers an unparalleled portrait of Darwin the social scientist, both in the range and originality of Darwin's thinking in what later became the fields of psychology, sociology, anthropology, and systems science. Loye's book will cause a revolution in social theory as diverse fields such as human ecology, urban studies, population dynamics, collective organization, and the study of culture and moral order are rethought and recast in the light of Darwin's moral theory. *Darwin's Lost Theory* is absolutely essential reading for every social scientist."

MEASURING EVOLUTION

Raymond Trevor Bradley, sociologist, Director, Institute for Whole Social Science, Carmel, CA, Associate Research Professor, BRAINS Center, Radford University, Radford, VA, author *Charisma and Social Structure: A Study of Love and Power, Wholeness and Transformation.*

※※※

"Since selfish gene theories are often linked to Charles Darwin, it is exciting to see a psychological theorist of Loye's quality and productivity argue that Darwin's own viewpoint was not that of the selfish gene theorists. Loye gets us into the heart of Darwin's works and shows that when it came to human evolution at least, love and connectedness were regarded not as anomalies but as intricately related to the entire evolutionary process. Altruism has for too long been explained away as just a devious form of selfishness, if not of one's own body then of one's genes. So have other common activities that make us human, such as the arts, religion, and creativity. Sexuality has been assumed to be motivated solely by reproductive needs, and its pleasurable and bonding aspects discounted, whereas Loye shows that Darwin saw sexual evolution as the primary basis of bonding and love in many animal species including our own.

"Loye's book will stimulate a dialogue that has hitherto been lacking, particularly in academia. Discussion of love, partnership, and concerns for the larger society has been largely absent from professional discussion of behavioral biology. This would be the first widely read book for a general educated audience that lays out the claims for a partnership-based approach to evolutionary and behavioral biology and ties such an approach to the originator of natural selection himself!

"*Darwin's Lost Theory* will fill an important gap. It will be a widely read and controversial book by an experienced and thoughtful author with style and flair. I expect it will become one of the major books of the early Twenty-First Century."

DAVID LOYE

Daniel S. Levine, theoretical psychologist and neural network theorist, author of *Introduction to Neural and Cognitive Modeling* and (forthcoming) *Common Sense and Common Nonsense*, psychology department, University of Texas at Arlington.

❋❋❋

"David Loye has passionately called our attention to a part of Darwin's work that not only significantly modifies his construction of natural selection, but does so more prominently in *The Descent of Man* than many other modifications scattered throughout his vast writings. Even a number of neoDarwinians are now getting ready to accept some version of what Loye identifies as Darwin's discovery of 'organic choice,' usually under the label of 'self-organizing processes.' I think Loye's work comes along at a propitious time."

Stanley Salthe, biologist and evolution theorist, author of *Development and Evolution* and *Evolving Hierarchical Systems*, Professor Emeritus, biology department, Brooklyn College of the City University of New York.

❋❋❋

"This book is a block-buster and an old paradigm smasher! I read it with a deep sense of its importance in balancing the biological reductionist myopia about our possible future and the evolution of our moral sentiments. Congratulations!"

Hazel Henderson, economics theorist and futurist, author of *Building a Win-Win World, The Politics of the Solar Age, Paradigms for Progress*, and *Creating Alternative Futures*.

❋❋❋

MEASURING EVOLUTION

"Loye's thesis is nothing less than revolutionary. In a carefully researched and beautifully written work, he dramatically changes our understanding of Darwin and of evolution itself."

Alfonso Montuori, former Chair of Graduate Studies, School for Consciousness and Transformation, California Institute of Integral Studies, Associate Editor, *World Futures: The Journal of General Evolution*, and author of *Evolutionary Competence*.

ABOUT THE AUTHOR

Behind the books of Darwin Anniversary author David Loye lies an unusual career path. While a very young news correspondent with the U.S.Navy in the closing years of World War II, he docked and roamed the same ports in South America that Darwin, as a similarly very young man, visited one hundred years earlier on the famous voyage of the Beagle. He became a television newsman during the Edward R. Murrow days. He wrote the national award-winning *The Healing of a Nation* and gained his doctorate in psychology in early middle age. While a Princeton and UCLA School of Medicine faculty member, he was the research director for major studies of political values, the use of the brain and mind in prediction, and the impact of movies and television on adults.

For the past twenty years he has been mainly involved with other scientists from around the world in development of the new fields of evolutionary systems science, chaos and complexity theory, and in studies of Darwin's life and works from these advanced new scientific perspectives. He is a co-founder of two international organizations for advanced evolution studies; a co-founder with his wife and partner—evolution theorist and well-known author of *The Chalice and the Blade,* Riane Eisler—of The Center for Partnership Studies; and founder of The

MEASURING EVOLUTION

Darwin Project (www.thedarwinproject.com), with a Council of more than 50 leading American, European, and Asian scientists, educators, and media activists.

Loye is the author of *The Leadership Passion, The Knowable Future, The Sphinx and the Rainbow, An Arrow through Chaos, Darwin's Lost Theory of Love*, and editor of *The Evolutionary Outrider: The Impact of the Human Agent on Evolution,* and *The Great Adventure: Toward a Fully Human Theory of Evolution.* Among publishers for his books are Norton, Wiley, Jossey-Bass, New Science Library, Park Street Press, Bantam Books, Delacorte, Praeger, Adamantine, Gordon & Breach, the State University of New York (SUNY Press), and publishers in Japan, China, Italy, the Netherlands, and three publishers in Germany.

His new six-book Darwin Anniversary cycle is the product of two decades of work with fellow members of the General Evolution Research Group, of which he was a co-founder, and the International Society of Systems Sciences on advanced studies of evolution. By the early 90s, Loye had uncovered Darwin's almost wholly unknown moral- and progressive action-oriented completion for his theory of evolution. His systems scientific reconstruction of the long ignored "rest of Darwin"—and its massive corroboration by progressive biologists and brain, social and systems scientists—has been hailed by leading scientists and other scholars as a major contribution to our understanding of Darwin, evolution, and the immense challenge facing our species in the 21st century (See Pre-Publication Reviews of *Darwin's Lost Theory* by Scientists and Educators in the closing documents for this book).

This new work—which brings to life a much larger and contradictory Darwin and the work of thousands of scientists building a hopeful and humanistic new expansion for the story and theory of evolution—first gained formal book publication in Germany and China. Then late in 2004, the second largest university press in America, State University Press of New York (SUNY Press), published *The Great Adventure: Toward a Fully Human Theory of Evolution.*

"In times like these a new worldview often arises at the margins of power, at the periphery of the action unfolding on the main stage," internationally known psychologist Mihaly Csikszentmihalyi writes in the foreword to this book by Loye with chapters by eleven other members of the General Evolution Research Group and The Darwin Project Council.

"The themes introduced by the authors are likely to be among the central ones of any new world-view... The organizing principle of the new faith—a faith of human beings about human beings—is evolution itself. Not the traditionally taught evolutionary scenario dominated by competition and selfishness, but an understanding closer to the original Darwinian one that sees cooperation and transcendence of the self as the most exciting parts of the story."

This is the story and the science that Loye unfolds in the six books of the Darwin Anniversary Book Cycle for the Benjamin Franklin Press (www.benjaminfranklinpress.com).

See The Darwin Anniversary and The Darwin Anniversary Book Cycle in the closing documents for this book—as well as the website for the new Darwin Anniversary Report (www.darwinanniversary.com)—for brief descriptions of Anniversary events and books.

www.ingramcontent.com/pod-product-compliance
Lightning Source LLC
LaVergne TN
LVHW091536060526
838200LV00036B/628